Software Configuration Management

COORDINATION FOR TEAM PRODUCTIVITY

ADDISON-WESLEY PUBLISHING COMPANY

Reading, Massachusetts • Menlo Park, California
Don Mills, Ontario • Wokingham, England • Amsterdam
Sydney • Singapore • Tokyo • Mexico City • Bogotá
Santiago • San Juan

Software Configuration Management

COORDINATION FOR TEAM PRODUCTIVITY

Wayne A. Babich
Wang Laboratories, Inc.

To my wife, Sue

Ada™ is a trademark of the U.S. Department of Defense,
Ada Joint Program Office.
UNIX™ is a trademark of AT&T Bell Laboratories.

Library of Congress Cataloging-in-Publication Data

Babich, Wayne A., 1952–
  Software configuration management.

  Bibliography: p.
  Includes index.
  1. Computer software.   I. Title.
QA76.754.B33   1986   005   85–22917
ISBN 0–201–10161–0

Preface

Sometimes it is embarrassing to be a computer programmer. What other profession has such a remarkable rate of schedule and cost overrun and outright failure? (It's rather like being an economist, except that we get better press.) Certainly, we would not be tolerant of structural engineers if half of all bridges were abandoned half-complete, and most of the rest were finished years behind schedule and then fell apart the first time a heavy truck drove over them.

Our failures are not of the individual contributors; most of us design, code, and debug adequately or even well. Rather, the failure is one of coordination. Somehow we lack the ability to take 20 or 30 good programmers and meld them into a consistently productive team. The purpose of this book is to help solve this problem.

Many of the techniques that are useful for coordinating a software team are much the same as techniques used for managing any sort of team project. This book does not discuss Pert charts, budget and schedule tracking, personnel management, or similar topics of a general nature that are adequately described in other references.

This book concentrates on a coordination problem that is peculiar to the software development business and is not well discussed elsewhere. I call this problem *software configuration management*.

The term *configuration management* derives from the

hard engineering disciplines (mechanical, electrical, industrial, etc.), which use change control techniques to manage blueprints and other design documents. The term *software* configuration management has traditionally been applied to the process of describing and tracking releases of software as the product leaves the development group for the the outside world. In particular, the U.S. military uses the term to describe its technique of controlling release of software from contractors.

I use the term in a more expansive sense. I include not just the formal release of software to the customer, but the day-to-day and minute-by-minute evolution of the software inside the development team. Controlled evolution means that you not only understand what you have when you are delivering it, but you also understand what you have while you are developing it. Control helps to obtain maximum productivity with minimal confusion when a group of programmers is working together on a common piece of software.

The book is directly addressed to first-line software project managers, senior programmers, and others who are charged with coordinating programming teams. It is equally useful for higher-level managers whose duties include software project management, as well as for nonsupervisory programmers who are assigned to build programming tools for other project members.

This book is also appropriate as supplemental reading for a university course in software engineering, such as might be given to seniors or graduate students majoring in computer science. Perhaps this material would be supplemented by two weeks' worth of lecture. (Maybe a discussion of these topics will minimize the "reality shock" experienced by new graduates when they leave academia for the real world.)

No particular programming language or other specific software expertise is assumed, although the reader will benefit most if his or her background includes work as a programmer on a team programming project. Many of the examples use Unix because of the popularity of that operating system, but no previous knowledge of Unix is assumed. The material presented is applicable to all types of programming, including data processing, applications, systems, and scientific.

The book is structured into three parts. The first six chapters discuss the principles and approaches that define the field of configuration management. Chapters 7 and 8 discuss configuration management issues related to two commercially available programming environments as examples of how the principles relate to the real world. Chapter 9 summarizes by presenting configuration management strategy for a hypothetical project.

The material is presented in a brief, easy-to-read manner, with no tables or graphs and absolutely no mathematics. I hope that readers can relax with the book after a hard day at the office, and maybe chuckle at some of the problems they suffered through during the day.

Very little of the material in this book is original thinking on my part. I would like to express appreciation to all of the people who taught me the lessons presented, particularly the people on the ALS team at SofTech, Inc. Reviewers who presented valuable advice include Larry Weissman, Applix, Inc.; Dick Quanrud, SofTech, Inc.; Ken Schroder, Bolt, Baranek & Newman; Steve Rakitin; Rich Simpson, Encore Computer; Rudy Bazelmans, Wang Laboratories; Nancy Martin, Softpert Systems; Philip Metzger; Stephen Fickas, University of Oregon; and Robert Babb, Oregon Graduate Center (and his students). SofTech, Inc. provided material resources toward the preparation of the manuscript, including computer time. Special thanks to Ed Tucker.

I invite your comments, criticisms, and contributions of "war stories."

Lowell, Massachusetts W.A.B.

Contents

9 APPLYING THE PRINCIPLES 130

RECOMMENDED READING 155

INDEX 159

Software Configuration Management

COORDINATION FOR TEAM PRODUCTIVITY

1

It is frustrating to work as a member of a large software development team. You can spend more time coordinating with (and tripping over) the other team members than you do programming. There is scarcely time left in the day for the design, coding, and debugging that constitute the real work of software development. Sometimes you feel as though you're only spinning your wheels.

This feeling is no illusion. The fact of the matter is that as the size of a project grows, productivity (defined as progress per working hour) declines. A team of eight does not produce twice as much as a team of four, and might actually produce less. The fall-off in productivity as team size increases is so dramatic that many medium-sized teams accomplish absolutely nothing—a particularly embarrassing situation.

The productivity problems of software teams are discussed by F. P. Brooks, Jr. in *The Mythical Man-Month* (Brooks 1975). Brooks observed that it is unrealistic to measure in "man months" the amount of work necessary to build software. A project that takes one person eight months is an eight man-month project, but it is not likely to be completed

Configuration Management

by two people in four months, or (worse yet) four people in two months.

Brooks attributes the productivity fall-off to the problems of communication between staff members. The more people involved, the more time is spent on communication among the staff members. On a three-person team, there are but three communication channels among the three people. But on a four-person team, there are six channels, as illustrated in Fig. 1.1.

Because the number of communication channels increases faster than the number of people involved, a large team spends proportionally more time communicating (and less time progressing) than a small team. As the team size increases, at some critical point all time is spent communicating and no time is left for real progress.

There can be no dispute that Brook's observations are correct. Like most insights, this one is obvious now that someone has thought of it. The unanswered question we must address is how we are going to use his insight to improve team productivity. Most software is too large to be built by one person, so we have to use teams. We need to

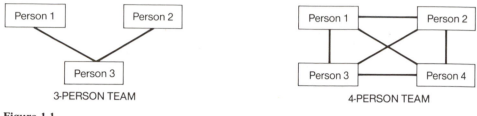

Figure 1.1

find ways to decrease the amount of time spent communicating and increase the time available for designing, coding,
and testing.

SYMPTOMS OF THE PROBLEM

Why is so much time spent communicating? What is all the
conversation about? Actually, conversation is not the big
time sink. The term *communication* is a little misleading; we
should use a more descriptive term: *coordination*. Programmers lose productivity because of the time they must spend
coordinating their work with that of the others. Even more
important, they lose productivity because of mistakes that
are made by *failing* to coordinate.

Consider some examples:

John has spent a week adding one of the new features
being readied by his team for a new software release. The
new feature requires modifications to six modules of the
system. He has tested the new feature and it works, but
when the completed release is turned over to the quality
assurance (QA) department, even the most trivial tests fail.
Somehow, not all six modules made it to QA in the form
John intended.

Marge is trying to find an obscure bug. She has narrowed
down the problem to a particular section of code and has
inserted all the necessary traces to find out what is happening. She is mystified because the source listing looks
correct, but the values produced by the traces are all
wrong. Finally, when she examines the load image with an

octal debugger, she discovers that the program listing she's been using doesn't match the code that she's debugging. When she finds the correct listing, the bug is obvious.

A software team is in the home stretch, conducting final debugging in preparation for a delivery at the end of the month. Suddenly, the staff comes in one morning and discovers that nothing works. The whole team grinds to a halt while the problem is traced to a typographical error that Dan made while performing a simple bug fix.

Aggravations such as these are daily occurrences in any software team. It's not hard to see why team programming is such a frustrating business and why productivity is a problem.

To solve the problem of team productivity, it is necessary to develop an understanding of where the lost time goes. It's all well and good to say that time is lost to coordination errors, but we are seeing only the symptoms, not the causes. To solve the problem, we need to describe the *nature* of the coordination errors. We must identify root causes of the errors and develop strategies to address them.

WHAT PROGRAM IS THIS?

It is possible to identify a common theme among the coordination problems faced by a software team. Programmers spend too much time trying to answer one question:

What program is this?

Although the theme itself is obscure (for it rarely arises in its bare form), the manifestations and disguises are familiar to anyone who has worked in software development.

"This worked yesterday. What happened?"

"I can't recreate the bug in this copy."

"What happened to the fix I put in last week?"

"The listing doesn't match the load image."

"Was that bug fixed in this copy, too?"

In all of these cases, the programmer is struggling to understand exactly which particular program is in hand. What state of progress does it represent? How is it different from other examples of the same program? The programmer spends valuable time trying to locate programs, understand exactly which copy of a program is needed, understand the differences between multiple copies or between what is in hand and what is needed.

In the earlier examples, John thinks he made changes to six modules and that all six modules were turned over to quality assurance. Maybe he was working on the wrong copies of the modules, maybe somebody else came along later and accidentally removed his changes, or maybe the wrong software was turned over to QA. Marge thought she was debugging a program that matched her listing, but she must have had either the wrong program or the wrong listing. Perhaps she was unaware of a change that was made after she produced her listing. Dan's team has to stop work to find out how today's nonworking software differs from the working software they left when they went home yesterday.

The essence of all these problems is coordination failure. To the people involved (staff and management alike), it feels like *confusion*. People are tripping over each other, forgetting to do something they meant to do, making changes that interfere with progress. Confusion diverts energy from the design, coding, and debugging that constitute the real work of software development. Confusion destroys morale and gives the staff a feeling of spinning their wheels.

The symptom of confusion might be that milestones are not met: It's taking two weeks to unit-test a certain subroutine when it should take only two days. (What really happened? It took two days to locate the most recent copy of the subroutine, two days of false starts with a supposedly debugged test driver, and four days of figuring out that somebody was changing copies of utilities called by the subroutine. *Then* it took two days to test the subroutine.)

The symptom of confusion might be that software is regressing, with more bugs today than yesterday. (What really happened? Somebody installed a "fixed" copy of a subroutine, erroneously resetting a data item that was supposed to be left around for a later phase. That somebody misunderstood the meaning of that data item.)

The symptom of confusion might be excessive turnover of the best people. (What really happened? It's so frustrating

Confusion diverts energy from the real work of software development.

to work on constantly shifting sands that the only alternative was to find another job.)

The symptom of confusion is certainly that time is slipping away—not in big increments, not in any pattern, but in an onslaught of individual incidents, each of which costs one or two programmers a couple of hours. Each slippage looks like an isolated incident. Each slippage won't happen again.

CONFIGURATION MANAGEMENT

On any team project, a certain degree of confusion is inevitable. The goal is to minimize the confusion so that more work can get done. The art of coordinating software development to minimize this particular type of confusion is called **configuration management.** Configuration management is the art of identifying, organizing, and controlling modifications to the software being built by a programming team. The goal is to maximize productivity by minimizing mistakes.

Configuration management can be applied to project materials other than software. The problem of team coordination is by no means limited to the question, "Which program is this?" When user's manuals are inconsistent or don't match software functions, customers might ask, "Which documentation is this?" Maintainers might find that test cases change mysteriously, or that bug reports remain open long after the bug is fixed. Managers might find that milestones are accomplished on schedule, but nobody can agree exactly *which* schedule was met. Just as multiple copies of software modules must be tracked, understood, and available, so iterations of budgets, specifications, design documents, interfaces, staffing plans, test reports, and all the other information the project creates and uses must be given the same attention.

Every software project should have someone assigned to be the configuration manager. On a project too small for the services of a fulltime configuration manager, the job can be combined with other responsibilities. The goal of the configuration manager is to spend time worrying about the question, "Which program is this?" so that nobody else has to.

THREE SAMPLE PROBLEMS

There are three typical problems that serve as examples of the need for configuration management:

- The double maintenance problem;
- The shared data problem; and
- The simultaneous update problem.

The Double Maintenance Problem

Double maintenance is the problem of keeping multiple identical copies of software.

The Monopolistic Industries DP staff has automated the payroll system and is now beginning to automate accounts payable. In 1983, Eric Promotable, chief programmer of the accounts payable project, discovers a utility package in the payroll system that formats, dates, and records checks, drives the special forms printer, and prepares for reconciliation with the bank statement. The software is fairly complicated and not trivial to build again, so Eric copies it for use in his own project. The accounts payable software now includes exactly the same code that is used in the payroll system, and at a savings of at least four work weeks. The accounts payable project is well on its way to success.

Next year, the accounts payable system is successfully delivered and in use for months. Wednesday, February 29, as the company prepares its end-of-month payment of bills, the computer operator is horrified to discover that all the checks coming off the printer are dated March 0, 1984. The check-formatting utility doesn't understand leap year. It takes more than a day to find and fix the error. The bug is in the code that Eric copied from the payroll system.

Quiz

1. Who will remember to fix the bug in the payroll system's copy of the check formatter?

2. If nobody remembers to fix the bug in the payroll system, what date will appear on the payroll checks that are printed Thursday night?

3. Is it likely that the fix that is put into the payroll system will exactly match the fix that was put into the accounts payable system?

The double maintenance problem is this: When there are two copies of the same software, then both copies need to be maintained. When a bug is found, someone needs to remember to fix it in both copies. Failing that, as in the preceding example, the bug surfaces independently in each copy, and it must be diagnosed and repaired twice. Even when people are instructed to make the fix in both copies, eventually someone will forget.

When a bug is fixed, not only must it be fixed in both copies, but it must be fixed *identically* in both copies. If the fixes differ even a little, then it is possible that the two copies might exhibit different behavior. With time, the multiple copies will differ more and more, and the multiplicity of maintenance will become more and more onerous. The two (supposedly identical) copies will soon become different, with bugs and "features" present in one and absent in the other.

The first principle of configuration management is to avoid multiple copies of the same information. In the real world of a team programming project, no amount of effort can ensure that two copies of identical information will be identical forever.

Multiple copies inevitably diverge.

The Shared Data Problem

The shared data problem arises when many people are simultaneously accessing and modifying the same data. The data might be program code.

In a particular real-time programming project, all of the source and object code for the multiple modules is stored on an online disk and shared among the project members.

Since there is only one copy of the source code, there is no double maintenance problem.

The software development is quite far along, with a large portion of the program integrated and working. Bill Barnstormer, crack software engineer, has a few bugs left in his input routines. Bill uses an editor to repair the bugs by editing the online source files. Then he recompiles the affected modules, creating new object code that overwrites the old.

Quiz

1. Can Bill pull this off without accidentally introducing a new bug?

2. When one of Bill's fixes turns out to be defective, in which module will the new bug manifest itself:
   - The input routines that Bill modified; or
   - In some other module that someone else is working on?

3. When other project members are trying to figure out why their code has suddenly stopped working, where will Bill be:
   - At his desk, waiting to fix the bug;
   - He'll be in late this morning; or
   - He resigned last week?

The shared data problem is this: When programmers are modifying a single copy of a program, then changes made by one programmer can interfere with the progress of others.

The most obvious case of interference is when the modification is wrong (i.e., a bad fix). Sometimes the modification will cause the entire software to crash, in which case everybody stops work until the bug is fixed. But sometimes the defect is subtle and shows up in a completely unexpected place that takes a long time to understand. In either case, the shared software doesn't work, and nobody can make any progress until the bug is repaired.

Even when a modification is valid, it might change the behavior of the program in ways that the entire programming team needs to understand. Perhaps the modification

Bill is sitting at his desk waiting to fix the bug.

changes the data displayed in a trace, or perhaps it changes the manifestations of an error. Perhaps a subroutine is passed arguments whose meanings are now slightly different.

Whatever the reasons, there are always going to be problems when programmers work together on one piece of source code. Regardless of how well programmers comunicate with each other, there will be times when changes introduced by one programmer are an unpleasant surprise to the others.

The Simultaneous Update Problem

Because of the shared data problem, a software team cannot comfortably work with one copy of the source code that everybody shares. But neither can each programmer have a personal copy of the program, or the double maintenance problem will be the penalty.

A simple (and common) solution is to divide the source code into a number of files called *modules*. A programmer who wants to modify a module makes a copy of it and changes the copy. The programmer then tests the change to make sure it is valid before making the change in the shared copy. The likelihood of team progress being spoiled by a defective fix is thereby minimized. Dan and Joan have adopted this approach.

Dan and Joan are both assigned to the enhancement of the database management software. Dan and Joan are aware of the shared data problem, so to avoid disrupting the other project members, they have wisely chosen to make personal copies of the modules they are working on. By making personal copies, they can make changes freely without interfering with other project members if they make a mistake. The personal copies can be rigorously tested to be sure they are working before the project's shared software is updated.

Joan is making a change to the representation size of integers, which requires a number of small changes to a variety of subroutines, so Joan copies from the shared project software the 20 subroutines she needs. She will be working on them for more than a week because of all the testing that is required. At the end of the week, she will copy the new versions of all 20 subroutines back into the project's shared copy.

Meanwhile, Dan is assigned to fix a number of little bugs. He makes a private copy of a subroutine, fixes its, tests it, and copies it back to the project's shared copy, all within a period of a couple of hours. He fixes two or three bugs a day.

The problem arises when Dan fixes a bug that coincidentally happens to be in one of Joan's 20 modules. Dan fixes the routine on Wednesday; then on Friday, Joan takes the private copy that she's been working on all week and copies it back into the shared copy. In doing so, Joan inadvertently overwrites Dan's fixes; the bug that Dan fixed once is now unfixed.

Joan and Dan ran into trouble because they were simultaneously updating the same module. Joan made a copy of a module, and while she was working on it, Dan made another copy so that he could do something different.

When two people are simultaneously updating the same software, one possibility is that one person's updates will be lost (overwritten), as Dan's was. A bug that was fixed yesterday suddenly becomes unfixed today. Another possibility is that the two fixes might conflict. Dan might be adding code that uses 16-bit integers at the same time that Joan is changing all integers to 32 bits.

An even worse case can arise when a programmer makes a change that spans multiple modules: Consider what might happen if some third programmer is simultaneously updating one of Joan's 20 subroutines that use the new representation size of integers so that Joan's modifications are lost in only that one subroutine. Nineteen subroutines use one representation size and one uses another. An error like this can take days (or weeks) to track down.

We seen to have a dilemma. If we keep multiple copies of software, we have the double maintenance problem. But if we keep one shared copy of the whole software project, the shared data problem is our penalty. If we try to get around the shared data problem by allowing people to make temporary copies of modules so that they may test without affecting others, then we find ourselves losing time because of the simultaneous update problem.

The three examples presented in this chapter are typical of the coordination problems that arise in any team software development. They provide a graphic explanation of the types of problems that fall into the general category of coordination failures. Solving problems like these is the concern of the configuration manager.

The following chapters present the principles behind solutions to these and other configuration management problems.

2

What is the purpose of a software development project? Some people might say that the purpose is to build a computer program, but the problem is harder than that. The purpose of a professional software development project is to build a *family* of computer programs. This chapter introduces the concept of a program family and discusses configuration management issues that arise when programs exist in multiple versions.

PROGRAM FAMILIES

No real-world software exists in only one version. Every product exists in alternative forms, successive releases, or custom-tailored adaptations for different environments. Every product exists in hundreds or even thousands of versions, the aggregate of which we call a *program family*.

Consider some examples of versions of a program:

A business graphics package needs to perform some floating-point computations (sin, cos, etc.) for construction of

Program Families

pie charts. The package is available on a microcomputer that can be equipped with an auxilliary floating-point processor. The graphics package is available in two versions: one version requires the auxilliary processor, and the other uses a software emulation of floating point. In this case, multiple versions are necessary to support alternative hardware configurations.

A program to perform computations of federal income tax withholding needs to be revised every year as the tax laws change. Each year a new version is released. In this case, multiple versions are necessary to support evolving functionality.

A word processing system is periodically revised to fix bugs detected by customers. Twice yearly, a new release is delivered. In this case, multiple versions are delivered to improve quality.

The purpose of a software development project is to build a family of computer programs.

A programming team is building a large piece of software. Rather than code the entire program and attempt to debug all at once, they chose to make a series of component builds. In the first version, just the input routines are present so that they alone may be tested. In each successive version, more of the subroutines are added (and tested), gradually building to the complete program. In this case, multiple versions of increasing levels of completion are used to facilitate debugging and testing.

A real-time program is designed to run on an embedded processor that has no human-readable I/O capabilities. Because it is difficult to debug on such a machine, a special version is prepared to run on a mainframe computer. By providing some small adaptations to the source code, and by adding some I/O scaffolding, it is possible to find most of the bugs on the mainframe, leaving much less debugging to be performed on the embedded processor. In this case, two versions are prepared to run on completely different computer hardware.

One respect in which professional software development differs from amateur programming is that production software must exist in multiple versions for all the reasons demonstrated in the preceding examples. In addition to these good reasons for multiple versions, multiplicity also exists through the forces of inadvertent software divergence. As the double maintenance problem shows, different versions of programs might exist simply because the programmer working on one copy of the software fixed a bug differently from the way the programmer working on another copy fixed it. Two copies that were formerly identical are now different versions.

The configuration management strategy must successfully control all the members of a program family to keep multiple versions identical in ways they are supposed to be identical and different in ways they are supposed to be different. Multiple versions must be controlled so that maintenance effort is minimized and unnecessary duplication of work is eliminated.

CONFIGURATIONS

Remember that it is the job of the configuration manager to worry about the question "What program is this?" Part of the job of the configuration manager is to understand and record the differences among versions of software and then be able to produce the correct version to fill a particular demand. How might the configuration manager keep track of all the different members of a program family?

The most obvious and common approach is to keep, for each version, the executable load image together with the source code and object code for the modules of which it is composed. Distinct physical media (disk pack, tape, or data area) are used for each version to avoid confusion about what is in the version. Figure 2.1 illustrates distinct media used to store two different versions of a program. The lettered boxes represent the modules of which the version is composed.

The problem with this approach is the double maintenance problem. It is to be expected that many of the modules present in one member of the family will also be present in other members. In the figure, modules A, B, D, E, and F are present in both versions and are therefore stored in two copies—one for each version of which they are a part. When a bug is discovered in one of these modules, the bug must be fixed in both places.

In general, there will be more than two versions of the software, and any given module might be in many places.

Figure 2.1

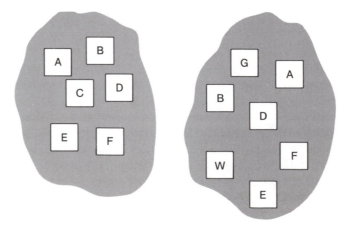

Every time a module is changed, it is necessary to locate all of the media on which the module is stored so that all copies may be repaired. Inevitably, the bug is not fixed in all occurrences of the module, or is fixed differently in some copies, and the multiple versions of software begin to differ in undesired ways.

To avoid this double maintenance problem, an alternative approach is used. This approach is to store in one place all the different modules used throughout the family, and, for each family member, keep a list of all the different modules of which any particular member is composed. See Fig. 2.2, in which the boxes represent modules. This general pool of modules is commonly called the *library*. Figure 2.2 shows that all the modules are stored together in one library. For each member of the program family, a list shows which modules are to be included in that version.

The list of modules of which a program is composed is called the *configuration* (hence the term *configuration management*). The figure shows the configuration of two different versions, named Version 1 and Version 2. Modules A, B, D, E, and F are present in both configurations.

Choosing which modules are to go into a particular program is called *configuring* the program, by analogy with computer hardware, in which a computer is configured from an assortment of options and peripherals.

Each module is present in only one place, so there is no double maintenance problem. If a module is to be a part of two versions, then it is referenced in two configurations, but it is never stored twice.

Figure 2.2

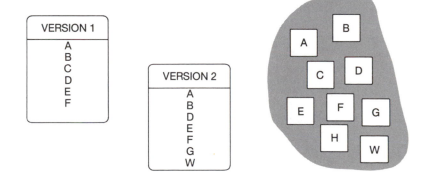

When it comes time to configure a new version of the program (i.e., create a new member of the program family), the programmer goes to the pool of modules and picks the relevant ones to link together (i.e., creates a new configuration). The process is much the same as configuring a meal from a Chinese restaurant menu (one from column A, one from column B).

For example, suppose someone wants to configure a program that produces output on a particular model of printer, supports the extended hardware floating-point options, and runs in 256K. The library might hold several different printer-output modules (one for each type of printer than is supported). There might also be two sets of floating-point utilities (hardware vs. software emulation), and two storage managers (disk based and memory based). The user would choose the printer-output module, the floating-point utilities, and the storage manager necessary to accomplish the goals.

Note that the library holds multiple versions of each module. When configuring a program, the programmer chooses the correct version of each module and links them together to form a complete program. In this way, a new configuration is formed by referencing the proper versions of modules that are present in the library.

The library must be properly organized to make it easy to create new configurations. The organization must reflect the relationships among the modules (for example, to show that the two different storage manager modules are alternatives to each other, one for large memory use and one for small memory use).

If a programmer is charged with creating a program that runs in 128K memory, handles three sensors, and uses the XY18A input device, it is essential that the programmer be able to find which version of module D is relevant. Alternatively, if a programmer working on an inventory control package wants to create a test configuration that has all the recent bug fixes relating to hierarchy of part numbers, but does not have the optimizations to the supplier-data retrieval, the programmer must be able to choose the correct versions of all the modules. The organization of the library is critical; it must reflect the differences among versions of a module. Proper library organization is a fundamental mechanism toward minimizing effort wasted discovering the answer to "Which program is this?"

The remainder of this chapter discusses the organization and representation of the modules in the library. If a module is to be present in a multitude of versions, then we must intelligently represent the versions. We need to understand the ways in which the versions differ and the ways in which they are the same so that we can easily choose the correct version for a particular configuration.

To discuss library organization properly, it is necessary to refine the concept of *version*. We must distinguish between two fundamentally different kinds of versions: *revisions* and *variations*. Revisions and variations are discussed in the following sections.

REVISIONS

Two versions of a module may differ because one is a *revision* of another. A revision is a new version intended to supersede the old. Revisions of a module commonly reflect progress in debugging the module, although they can also reflect added functionality or performance improvement. The library might contain many revisions of each module, reflecting the evolution of the module. Each revision introduced into the library should have fewer bugs or in some other way be better than the earlier revisions. The intention of the creator is that the newest revision will make the older ones obsolete.

Note that we can refer to older and newer (even newest) revisions. Revisions come in a linear order, related to the time sequence in which they are created. They might be numbered, with 1 being the oldest (or first) revision. The intention is that revision $N+1$ supersedes revision N and all earlier revisions.

The library is organized to show that the multiple versions of each module are a set of revisions. Naming or numbering conventions are used to show this relationship and the ordering from oldest to newest. Figure 2.3 shows that the library contains four revisions of module A, named A(1), A(2), A(3), and A(4). The revisions are illustrated as a stack of cards, with the oldest at the back and the newest at the front.

The question might be asked: If the newest revision is intended to supersede the older ones, why are the older ones kept in the library? Why aren't they simply discarded?

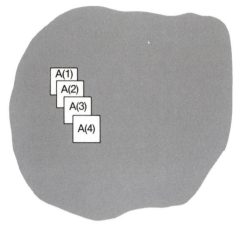

Figure 2.3

There are many reasonable and essential uses for an older revision N, even when the newer revision $N+1$ is available. One reason is that despite the intentions of the programmer who created it, revision $N+1$ might not be better than revision N. Perhaps revision $N+1$ has more bugs than revision N. Even if $N+1$ has fewer bugs, its bugs may not be a subset of the bugs in revision N (e.g., three bugs fixed, one new one created).

An equally important reason for saving older revisions is that they may be needed to reproduce bugs that are present in older software. Even if revision $N+1$ does only fix bugs, it might be necessary to reference an older revision to replicate a bug reported from the field, or for other purposes, to know that you have exactly the same software you had yesterday. Chapters 3 and 5 contain extensive discussions on this subject.

VARIATIONS

A library might contain multiple versions of a module that are *variations* of each other. Module variations fulfill the same function for slightly different situations and are therefore intended to be alternative, interchangeable parts. A configuration typically includes only one variation of any given module.

Unlike revisions, new variations do not supersede old. Multiple variations coexist as equal alternatives. Variations are named, not numbered, because there is no meaningful linear order among them. The name of a variation reflects the purpose it serves, not the order in which it was created.

There are many reasons why a library might include multiple variations of a module. One reason is that alternative variations might support different types of hardware. There might be four variations of the printer-output module, one for each model of printer supported. A configuration will reference the appropriate variation for the hardware that needs to be supported.

Figure 2.4 illustrates a library that includes four variations of the printer support module, one for each model of printer.

The variations are illustrated as coequal alternatives implementing a *variation set*. The hexagon header in the illustration is not itself a module, but is a notational mechanism for showing the organization of the variation set. In this example, the modules are named PrintOut(Ep6), PrintOut(Ep5), PrintOut(Db3), and PrintOut(Ald); the name of the printer model appears inside the parentheses. The naming convention is an important tool for describing the relationship among the variations.

There are reasons for variations other than hardware differences. A library might include multiple variations of a module to fulfill alternative functionalities. In a payroll sys-

Figure 2.4

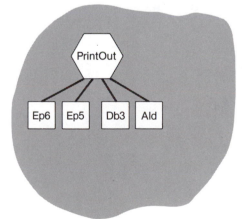

tem, multiple variations of the state-tax withholding module might exist to reflect the differences in the tax laws of each state. In a building security system, alternative variations might describe the different floorplans on each floor of the building.

Sometimes a library contains module variations that exist only for purposes of testing and debugging. One special variation of a module might include traces, assertions, and data dumps designed to aid debugging. Another example of a variation used only during program development is a *stub*. A *stub* of a module is a variation that does nothing, but does it gracefully (without crashing). Programmers might build a configuration that references stubs of those modules they do not want to test. By including a stub rather than a fully implemented variation, they can test code without running the risk of being blocked by bugs other than the ones they are seeking.

We have seen that there are two different kinds of versions: revisions (which are linearly ordered) and variations (which are equal alternatives). All versions of a module are related to each other by being either revisions or variations. The organization of the library explicitly reflects these relationships.

Typically, there are both variations and revisions of a single module. With time, each variation will require bug fixes and performance improvements, resulting in multiple revisions of each variation. Figure 2.5 shows that one of the printer-output variations has been revised.

Figure 2.5

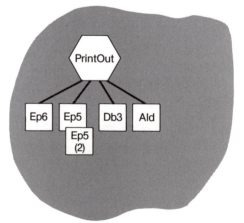

STORING VERSIONS OF MODULES

Every module is present in the library as a set of versions of that module. The versions are related to each other as revisions and variations. How are all these versions of a module stored?

Separate Files   Typically, each of the versions of a module is stored in its own file. The source code for one version is in one file, and the source code for another version is in another file. Naming conventions are used to record the fact that the two files represent different versions of the same module. In Fig. 2.6, the two variations of the memory management module are stored as two distinct files: one variation for 128K that stores all data in main memory, and one variation for 64K that spills excess data out to disk as necessary.

The problem with this approach is that old bugaboo, the double maintenance problem. When a bug is uncovered in the 128K variation, it might also exist in the 64K variation, in which case it must be fixed a second time there. Furthermore, it must be fixed in an identical way or the two variations will differ unnecessarily. How do we prevent unnecessary divergence of the variations? In the long run, we don't.

Keeping both versions up-to-date can be complicated. Since the two variations are different (if they weren't we would not have two variations), how do we know that a bug

Figure 2.6

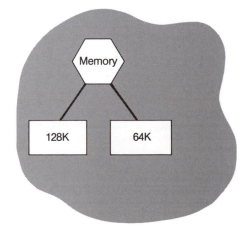

discovered in the small-memory variation exists in the large-memory variation? The bug may be in a portion of the code that is intended to be different. And even if the bug does exist in both variations, what leads us to believe that it is possible to apply the identical fix?

Deltas   An alternate approach to storing each version separately is to store a single full version and to represent the other versions by their differences from the one. The differences are called *deltas*. We might store the 128K variation in a file, then separately store the delta that transforms the 128K variation into the 64K variation. The 64K variation is not itself stored in a file. Figure 2.7 shows that the library contains the 128K variation and a delta that produces the 64K variation.

The delta file contains a complete description of the differences between the two variations. Typically it contains editing commands that describe exactly what statements to add at exactly what place to transform the 128K variation into the 64K variation. In this case, the delta shows that, at a particular place in the algorithm, certain code must be added to check for overflow of memory and spill out to disk if necessary. If we want to read the 64K variation, we retrieve the 128K variation and *apply the delta* (i.e., make the transformation), which yields the 64K variation. Note that it is possible to use either version as the original. If the 64K variation were the original, then the delta would show that the disk-spill code should be removed to create the 128K variation.

Figure 2.7

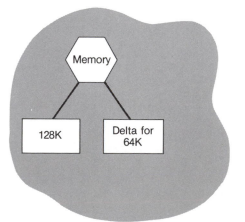

The advantage of the delta approach is that when a bug is fixed in the original (128K) variation, it is not necessary to fix the bug again in the other variation. Since the delta shows only the differences, anything that is common is automatically preserved when the delta is applied.

Another important advantage of deltas is that they are economical in their use of disk storage space. Much less space is consumed by one original and 23 deltas than is consumed by 24 separate versions.

The disadvantages of deltas are subtle but very real. One important disadvantage is that if for some reason the original file should be lost or corrupted, then the entire set of versions is lost. Lacking the original, it is not possible to create any variation with just the delta alone. A regular backup procedure, carefully followed, minimizes this risk.

Another important drawback to deltas is the complication involved in representing transformations. A simple way of representing deltas is by reference to line numbers. A delta might specify, for example, that certain new lines are to be added after line 52 in an original file. Such a scheme fails if the original file is modified. For example, if a delta shows that the original is to be modified by adding certain text after line 52, and if the original is changed so that a new line is added between lines 10 and 11, then the delta is no longer correct and needs to be updated to show that the code is to be added after line 53. If you make the change at line 52, it will be in the wrong place. For this reason, more sophisticated algorithms are necessary when deltas are used to represent variations, in which case the original variation is subject to frequent modification.

Deltas are a good method for representing revisions of modules. The original is revision number 1. A series of deltas represents the transformations from revision 1 to revision 2, then from revision 2 to revision 3, and so on. Since early revisions are not typically modified, simple algorithms can be used to store deltas using references to line numbers. Unlike variations, revisions are commonly represented using deltas, primarily for the purpose of saving disk space.

When deltas are used to represent revisions, it is possible to use either *forward* or *reverse* deltas. Forward deltas start with the oldest revision and use deltas to show the transformations from revisions N to revision $N + 1$. Reverse deltas start with the most recent revision and represent transformations from each revision N to revision $N - 1$. Reverse deltas have the advantage that the most recent revision is immediately available without any computation necessary to apply deltas. If forward deltas are used, then it is necessary to apply all of the deltas to get from the oldest to the most recent revision. Since the recent revisions are accessed more often than the older ones, reverse deltas are an optimization of retrieval effort. Reverse deltas, however, have the drawback that the most recent revisions might be subject to change, which would require recreation of the deltas.

Conditional Compilation   A third approach to representing the versions of a module is to represent all the versions using one copy of source code and take advantage of conditional compilation to represent the differences. Source code that is relevant to only some versions is bracketed by macro commands so that the compiler can recognize which statements are relevant for which versions. When the compiler is invoked, it is told which version of object code is to be produced. It automatically ignores source statements that are not part of the proper version.

The advantage to conditional compilation is that shared code is represented only once, so fixes to the code are effective for all versions. Therefore, there is no double maintenance problem.

Another important advantage is that conditional compilation avoids the combinatorial explosion that can result if the module is varied for multiple reasons. For example, if a particular module must support three types of input devices and four types of output devices, then it must exist in $3*4 = 12$ variations. If distinct files are used, then 12 files are required; if deltas are used, then an original plus 11 deltas are required. But if conditional compilation is used, the source code will probably contain three conditionally bracketed sections of code for input and four conditionally bracketed sections of code for output, with no multiplicative effect.

Conditional compilation can be an effective scheme until the differences between versions become so complex that the source code is impossible to read. For this reason, conditional compilation is used primarily to store variations, not revisions. Differences among variations are typically localized and stable, as contrasted with the random nature of bug fixes. If conditional compilation were used to store revisions, the complexity of the source code would soon become unmanageable for the human reader.

Like the delta approach, conditional compilation is vulnerable to loss of all versions if the one file is lost.

Chapters 7 and 8 show examples of two alternative configuration management systems that represent revisions and variations. The Unix™ Revision Control System uses deltas, whereas the Ada™ Language System uses distinct files.

3

The question "What program is this?" arises most frequently during debugging. Debugging traditionally involves an analysis of what the program does, performed by either reading the source code or observing its execution. But many times the fastest approach to finding a bug is not analysis of the program itself, but analysis of the *history* of the program—how it was created. The history of the program is called its *derivation*. This chapter discusses the recording of program derivations and the use of derivations to find bugs and the proper program to debug.

THE PURPOSE OF DERIVATIONS

The essence of debugging is to discover how the execution of a program differs from what is desired. It's usually possible to debug by examining the algorithms or the outputs and deducing what must have happened. But sometimes the most expeditious approach is not to examine the program itself, but rather to ask questions about the history of the program.

A software team is integrating the components of a process control system one component at a time in a series of builds. After each component is added, the whole system is subjected to regression tests to make sure no errors have crept in. Only when the current build passes all tests is the next component added.

One day, after a particular build has been successfully tested, a new output module is added. Suddenly a much earlier computation module crashes. The new output module "couldn't possibly" be causing that bug. Is the impossible happening? Or is some other sinister force at work?

Odds are that the process control team will discover absolutely nothing by examining the source listings of the output module. After all, the module successfully passed all its unit tests before it was submitted for integration. Besides, how could it be that the output module is causing the computation module to crash even before the output module is called?

Perhaps an examination of the history of the new build will reveal the problem. Maybe someone coincidentally substituted a new revision of the computation module at the same time the output module was added, in which case the bug has nothing to do with the output module. Possibly the history might reveal that storage was reallocated to make room for the new module, in which case the computation module data has been moved to another overlay.

> A bug has recently appeared in a file-update module of a data processing application. The module is large and complicated and hasn't been touched for months. Nobody knows quite where to begin looking for the problem.

Before the data processing team begins detailed analysis of the file-update module, they might find the problem just by asking a few questions. Perhaps a new compiler version has recently been introduced, and the file-update module was never recompiled. Or perhaps the direct-access I/O package, which is used heavily by file update, has just been modified to add some new features.

Note that the answers to these questions will likely be all that is needed to locate a mysterious bug. Think of all the analysis that might be necessary to find the bug if there were not sufficient information to answer the questions. Analyzing the derivation is often a far faster way to find a bug than is analyzing the code.

An ounce of derivation is worth a pound of analysis.

The common element in these examples is that the easy solution to the problem requires a knowledge of what went into the problem software—its derivation. Effective configuration management requires the accurate recording of derivations.

Let's see how a good derivation might be used to solve the problem of the process control program:

> Yesterday's build passed all its tests, so the output module was added overnight. Today, the program blew up in an earlier computation phase. Why did the addition of the output module cause an error in an unrelated earlier phase?

The derivation of today's build lists the names of all the object code that was linked together to form the executable image, including the exact revision and variation of each module. A programmer can compare the derivations of yesterday's and today's builds and see that the computation module is in fact the same today as it was yesterday, so no new errors could have been introduced there. But today's double-precision library contains a higher-numbered revision of the multiplication routine; perhaps that is the source of the problem.

The new revision of the double-precision multiplication routine has a derivation history that describes the nature of its difference from yesterday's revision. It says that a new argument was added to the multiplication routine so that overflow errors can be reported. This argument was added so that the output module would know when to print a row of asterisks instead of a spurious number caused by overflow.

Because today's computation module is identical to yesterday's, we can conclude that the computation module has not been upgraded to conform to the new argument-passing conventions of the double-precision multiplication routine. The computation module is passing too few arguments to the double-precision multiplication routine; the crash in the computation module is therefore caused by a change to the double-precision multiplication routine. The bug has been found, but not one line of code has been examined.

RECORDING DERIVATIONS

If a derivation is to be useful, it must be precise.

In the process control example, the debugging process requires that the derivation show exactly which modules were linked to form a build. It wouldn't be much help if the only information available were that the double-precision multiplication module is indeed linked into the builds; what the team needs to know is which *revision* of the multiplication module is linked into today's build, and which revision was linked into yesterday's. It's good to know, for example, that a given program is derived by linking modules A, B, and C. But are we talking about module C before or after Joe tightened the code to speed it up? Was module A compiled with that old compiler, or did we remember to recompile it after we received the new compiler? Which overlay structure did we use when we linked A, B, and C? The derivation must be precise.

A precise derivation of a program or module requires:

1. An identification of the tool that created it; for example, which linker or which compiler;
2. An identification of the data that was input to the tool; for example, which source code was fed to the compiler;
3. An identification of the options and arguments given to the tool; for example, which overlay structure, or which compiler options;
4. The reason why that particular data, arguments, and options were given to the tool;
5. The person who was responsible for creating the data; and
6. The date and time.

Consider an example of a comprehensive derivation of a module of object code:

Produced 15:18 6/19/85 by FORTRAN MV compiler version 3.20

Source input: TtyFormat revision 15.2

Referencing included file TtyCommon revision 3.0

Options: OPTIMIZE = SPACE, FLOAT = NOFLOAT, ERRLEVEL = 2

Recompiled by Joe to reference new revision of TtyCommon

This derivation identifies the tool, the input, the options, the person, and the reason. The input files used by the FORTRAN MV compiler are the source code (TtyFormat) and another text file that was referenced with an include macro (TtyCommon). Joe created this object code because he wanted a version that referenced the new revision 3.0 of TtyCommon.

If a mysterious bug is identified in the TtyFormat module, a programmer reading the derivation might realize that:

■   Revision 3.0 of TtyCommon was the wrong revision to include;

- ERRLEVEL 2 prevents compiler diagnosis of a particular error condition that might be causing the bug;
- Use of OPTIMIZE = SPACE with version 3.20 of the compiler has a known bug related to the handling of common size larger than 1024 bytes; or
- The MV compiler was the wrong compiler to use.

In all these error situations, analysis of the source code of the TtyDriver module would reveal nothing. Adding traces or using an interactive symbolic debugger requires days of work. But the derivation can be used to find the bug because it contains the detailed history of the object code. In the worst case, the derivation points to Joe as someone who might be able to give suggestions to help find the problem.

A derivation should be kept for every file used by the programming team. This includes source code, object code, and executable images (as well as documentation, schedules, budgets, etc.). In the preceding process control example, the bug is found, not from an examination of one derivation, but by following a chain of derivations from the build down to the source code. (See Fig. 3.1.)

The derivation of the build names the object code that was linked together. A comparison of the derivations of today's vs. yesterday's object code for the double-precision library shows that today's represents a new revision of source code for the multiplication routine. The derivation of the source code for the multiplication routine contains the reason for the new revision, which is the information necessary

Figure 3.1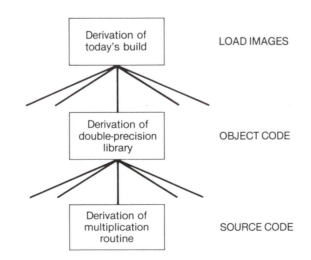

to understand the error. Each file (load image, object code, source code) has attached to it a derivation; each derivation references other files, and thereby other derivations, producing a genealogy that can be traced until the error is found.

The derivations of load images, object code, object libraries, and so on, consist primarily of references to files. The derivation of a load image, for example, includes the names of object code that was linked together.

A precise (and therefore useful) derivation depends on strict control of file names. If module A is undergoing periodic modification to fix bugs, it is not sufficient to identify all the different stages simply as A. They could be named A(1), A(2), and so on, or they could be named A from Dec. 3, 1985, A from Dec. 5, 1985, and so on, but they must be distinguished.

An essential principle of configuration management is that *file names must never be reused*. The naming convention must distinguish between different versions so that every name is unambiguous. If a file is modified, then a new version has been created and must receive a new name. No two different files may share the same name because a derivation is only as good as the names of the files it references.

If you change a file, change its name.

The derivation of human-readable files, such as source code and documentation, includes an explanation of the reason the file was created and an emphasis on the differences between this file and other versions. When programmers create a new version of source code for a module, they record in the derivation the version they started with and the motivation and details of the changes they made.

A common convention is to use comments to create a *change log* at the top of each source file, as shown in Fig. 3.2. The first paragraph placed into the change log describes the creation of the first version of the module. Every time programmers make a change (thereby creating a new version), they add a new paragraph to the top of the change log. When read from bottom to top, the change log is a history of all the changes that have been applied. Changes are added to the top (rather than the bottom) of the log because of the presumption that the most recent changes are of greatest interest.

```
/* CHANGE LOG


4. RKJ 6/7/85                                          Bug Rpt 317
   Corrected end condition of central loop in RKPUT_ANSWER.
   Test should be against COUNTER-1, not against COUNTER
3. RKJ 5/28/85                                         Bug Rpt 272
   Added third argument to RKTEST_VALUE to pass back value
   indicating the nature of the error. Corrected all calls to
   provide corresponding third actual parameter.
2. JBB 4/4/85                                          Bug Rpt 223
   Created new subroutine RKTEST_VALUE to check for correct
   value of descriptor type. Added call to this routine from
   three places in RKPUT_ANSWER.
1. RKJ 3/13/85                                         Bug Rpt 198
   New module created to prepare output formatting for
   advanced descriptor types. This function formerly
   performed incorrectly in the general descriptor-type
   output module, failing to distinguish descriptors of
   class Env.



               END OF CHANGE LOG */
```

Figure 3.2

If each entry in the change log is numbered (as in Fig. 3.2), then changes to the actual source code can be accompanied by comments that refer to the number corresponding to the change. The definition for the subroutine RKTEST_VALUE, for example, includes a comment referencing change log entry 3, in which the third argument is added to the parameter list.

A common mechanism for emphasizing changes between the current and previous revisions of a file are *change bars*. A change bar is a vertical line that appears in the left or right margin to designate a line that is different or new in this revision and distinguishes it from the previous revision of the file. Change bars do not show that lines have been omitted, nor do they describe the nature or purpose of the change within a line. Change bars can be used on source code only if the compiler can be instructed to ignore them as part of the program syntax. For this reason, change bars are normally used in documentation rather than in source code.

Figure 3.3 shows nested change bars. Lines with only one bar are different between this revision (*N*) and the previous (*N* − 1). Lines with two bars, however, are different between *N* − 1 and *N* − 2 and are therefore one revision removed.

```
Module UPGRADE_CLASS
This module upgrades the fare class of passengers that
meet at least one of the following criteria:
   - active duty military officer
   - corporate account with minimum 20% class B-C or B-D
fare discount structure
   - diplomatic passport from allied country
   - active or retired corporate executive with grade level
of 23 or higher.
```

Figure 3.3

REPRODUCIBILITY

A derivation can be an immensely useful tool for debugging. But, clearly, it does not solve all problems. Often you must analyze the executable software with more traditional techniques, such as an interactive debugger or traces. In these cases, you must obtain an executable program that displays the bug. This is not as easy as it sounds.

If the software product exists in only a few releases, you can keep a copy of each. When a bug is reported, you can go to the tape library and retrieve the release against which the bug was reported.

This approach doesn't work when the program exists in a large variety of configurations. Imagine a company that sends out a monthly list of system patches to each customer; each customer is free to adopt the patches that seem relevant. The company cannot keep a library large enough to hold configurations consisting of every possible combination of patches. The only reasonable approach is to create the proper program as needed, using the customer's report stating which release was used and which patches have been installed. The customer's report is the derivation of the software that displays the problem. The program that is at the customer's site is recreated in-house using the derivation supplied by the customer. So now we see another use for derivations: The derivation can be used to reproduce the software. The derivation shows the tool to use, the inputs that are necessary, and the options that should be specified to reproduce the software.

The ability to recreate software is particularly useful when each copy of a program is custom configured according to customer site requirements. (Each customer has a program slightly different from any other customer.) The ability

to recreate a configuration is also useful during initial program integration, when the program being tested may change daily. In both situations, it isn't practical to keep every configuration that ever existed.

To recreate exactly a given piece of software, it is necessary to have a detailed derivation: exactly which tool to use; exactly which input data; exactly which options and arguments. But more is necessary: it is necessary to be able to find the inputs.

All the detailed derivations in the world are worthless if you have lost the necessary input data. What good is it to know that you must link in the revision of module A from before Harvey tuned it, if Harvey threw away that revision as soon as the new one was tested? Reproducibility of software is a harder problem than is merely keeping precise derivations.

If a tool or input is listed in the derivation history of something you want to be able to recreate, you must prevent it from being either deleted or modified. Files for which deletion and modification are forbidden are called *frozen*. To use derivations to recreate software, the following principle must be enforced.

Anything that appears in a derivation must be frozen.

The concept of freezing includes both immutability and protection against deletion. Immutability is a general requirement of configuration management and is a corollary of the rule, "If you change a file, change its name." But protection against deletion is a stronger condition, necessary only if you intend to use the file to reproduce software.

Protection against deletion implies use of a large amount of storage space. You might infer that if you want to be able to reproduce any software that ever existed, you have to save every piece of source code that ever existed (every revision and every variation). That seems to be an overwhelming undertaking that requires vast quantities of magnetic media.

If isn't necessary, of course, to recreate every transient piece of software that ever existed, so not everything needs to be saved. And many files that need to be preserved can migrate to an offline *archive*, carefully organized for ease of retrieval, but stored on tape, floppies, write-once disks, or other inexpensive media. Even considering these factors, comprehensive freezing for reproducibility involves less storage space than would be expected. Why is this? The answer lies in the informal mechanisms that programmers develop to protect themselves from mistakes.

In a programming environment in which source code is frozen for reproducibility, a large amount of information is saved, but it is saved only once, as part of a comprehensive configuration management scheme. In a less controlled environment, each programmer feels the need for protection against the possibility of defective fixes, or against the possibility of needing to recreate an old configuration. Programmers save whatever information they think they might need, rather than depend on the programming system to do it for them. The result is wasted space due to redundant storage of data.

The need for reproducibility exists regardless of whether an organized configuration management scheme is provided. If no configuration management strategy exists, programmers develop *ad hoc* techniques for themselves. If data is not saved in a central location, it will be saved in multiple locations. If it is not saved in an organized archive, it will be saved online by default.

Even though large amounts of storage space are needed for controlled reproducibility, even larger amounts of storage space may be needed for uncontrolled reproducibility.

4

In 1971, David Parnas (Parnas 1971) proposed a new principle of software engineering. Loosely interpreted, his principle states that software development proceeds more rapidly when the programmers understand as little as possible of what each other is doing. Though considered radical at the time, the principle, called *information hiding*, now forms the backbone of our understanding of the software design process.

This chapter discusses information hiding and modular design as applied to the problem of software configuration management. Effective configuration management becomes much easier when the software is designed according to Parnas' principles. Changes are fewer and less coupled, and versions of modules are more nearly interchangeable.

INFORMATION HIDING

Intuition tells us that a team works best when each member has a thorough understanding of the work the others are doing. Unfortunately, intuition does not always serve us well. The fact is that for many aspects of software development, minimal understanding is the path to maximum progress.

Interfaces

Consider an example:

Max Performance is a member of a team developing an inventory management system. He is responsible for the module that controls allocation of the shelf space in the warehouse.

Max's module makes frequent access to the parts-description database, particularly for the quantity-in-stock information stored there. The database is accessed through special database-inquiry functions, built by Debby, another project member. When Max needs to know the quantity in stock of a particular part, he calls Debby's inquiry functions, passing the part number as an argument.

Max suspects that the multiple calls he is making to the database management routines will slow his code dramatically; he estimates that nearly 10% of the time consumed by his module will be wasted in calls to the database manager. Clearly, it is appropriate to bypass those slow routines and directly access the appropriate fields in the database.

Max redesigns his module to access the disk file that contains the database, going directly to the necessary fields without using the slower general purpose inquiry functions Debby has provided. Debby is happy to explain to Max how the file is laid out on disk so that Max can write his code.

It doesn't take much imagination to figure out what's going to happen to Max and Debby. Every time Debby makes a change to the physical structure of the database, she will not only have to modify her own inquiry functions, but also tell Max so he can modify his own special purpose access.

For a while Max and Debby will be able to coordinate their activities successfully. Every time Debby has to add a new field, she will tell Max and Max will make the changes. But eventually Debby will forget to tell Max, or Max will forget to make the change, and the software will stop working. Or maybe Debby will need to make a change and Max will tell her that she can't, because he's busy on something else and cannot update his software right now. Eventually Max and Debby will lose their cool, and the project manager will be invited to arbitrate. Debby's case might go like this:

"I didn't tell him that I was changing the supplier pointer because I didn't think he was using it. That's got nothing to do with quantity in stock. It's not my fault."

Max and Debby have gotten themselves into a permanent maintenance nightmare. The problem is compounded if there are more people who want direct physical access to the database, and compounded again as staff turns over and new programmers are brought into the maintenance effort. The project manager will get sick of hearing whose fault it's not.

Max and Debby's problem is a classic double maintenance problem. The knowledge of the physical database structure is present in two places (Max's module and Debby's functions). When one is changed, the other must be changed. Divergence (and, therefore, error) is inevitable. The problem is that Max knows too much about how Debby's software works. Max should be calling Debby's database management functions; he should not be attempting to understand (much less depend on) the physical structure she is building. The knowledge of the physical structure should be contained only in one place: Debby's functions. If Max knew less about what Debby was doing, the problems wouldn't arise. In fact, Max's goal of improved system performance might even be better served because Debby would have more freedom to revamp her database structure for improved access speed.

The theory behind information hiding is that the correct operation of one module should depend as little as possible on the details of the operations of other modules. When it is necessary to change a module, it should not be necessary to change other modules. The fix should be localized. The principle of information hiding is a restatement of the evils of double maintenance.

A programmer who understands the details of code other people write is apt to write code that is dependent on those details in a way the other programmers didn't anticipate. (Debby did not anticipate that Max would use the supplier pointer.) When the details of one person's code change, the other code ceases to work. A web of interdependence produces unnecessary bugs as maintenance progresses.

Asking each programmer to understand the whole to write a portion is an invitation to bugs. Asking each programmer to understand how the whole evolves during maintenance is wasteful of programmer time and brainpower. Minimal understanding leads to maximum progress.

INTERFACES

How can the principles of information hiding be applied to software development? The answer is to divide the software into pieces so that each programmer can work on one piece without understanding anything about how other programmers are building their pieces. Since all the pieces need to work together in the end, such a strategy requires careful planning. This planning is called *design.*

The path to maximum progress is to divide the total software into modules, each module relating to the others in a precisely defined way. The purpose of each module as it relates to all the other modules is called its *interface.* The way that the module accomplishes its purpose is its *implementation.* The implementation is not part of the interface. The logical separation between interface and implementation is essential.

The interface of a module describes everything that the author of another module needs to know about the operation

of the first. The author of any given module need understand
only the interfaces between that module and the others, and
need not understand the implementation of any other module. If each module meets all of its interfaces exactly, then
it will integrate smoothly with all other modules. In this way,
we constrain what the programmer has to understand about
what the other programmers are doing. The interface is like
the tip of the iceberg—though it's a small part, it's the only
part anyone sees (see Fig. 4.1).

Since the author of a module knows only the interfaces
(not the implementations) of the other modules, the code the
author writes does not need to be modified when the implementation of another module changes. It might be necessary
for another author to reimplement another module completely. The first author's code, however, will not need modification. When an implementation is changed, it is changed
in only one place and no other modules need be modified.
The double maintenance problem has been eliminated by the
separation of interface from implementation.

In the example of Max and Debby, Debby's database
manager is a module that interfaces with Max's module, providing services to retrieve data. The physical structure of the
database is part of the implementation of the database manager and is therefore not available to Max. When it is necessary to access the database, Max's module calls Debby's
inquiry function, which provides the interface between the
two modules. When Debby needs to modify the physical
structure, she modifies the implementation, and Max is unaware of the change. If there are performance problems, they
can be addressed by tuning the database management strategies.

Figure 4.1   *The interface is like the tip of the iceberg.*

A well-defined interface is useful to both the original author of the module and any future author (e.g., a maintainer). When a future author is fixing a bug, improving performance, or for some other reason modifying the database manager module, that author knows that as long as conformity with the interface is maintained, modifications will not have any detrimental effect on the operation of any other module. The interfaces to each module describe every characteristic upon which other modules depend. The database manager can be successfully maintained without any understanding of Max's shelf-space allocation code.

When a module is built to strictly defined interfaces, then all of the revisions and variations are interchangeable. Consider the example of Chapter 2, in which a printer-output module is available in a number of different variations to support a variety of printers. Each variation will obey the same interface, but the implementations will differ to reflect the characteristics of the hardware. Since all variations obey the same interface, the other modules that call for printer output do not know with which printer-output variation they are linked. All variations of the module are invoked the same way so they may be interchangeably included in a configuration.

Had the printer-output variation not obeyed a well-defined interface, then a module that calls one variation of printer output might not work with other variations. The problem of composing a valid configuration would then be considerably more difficult.

We now see why the principles of information hiding predict that maximum progress is made when the authors of each module understand nothing of the other modules except their interfaces to them.

But, the real-world solution is not as simple as this discussion suggests. In the real world, there are bugs, staff turnover, and tight deadlines. The author of a given module must understudy other programmers to help find bugs in their code. Having only one person who understands a critical portion of code creates unnecessary management exposure. Although Max must not write code that depends on the implementation of the database manager, it would be helpful if he understood enough to help Debby by reviewing her design or proofreading her code. And if Debby gets hit by a truck or (worse yet) falls behind schedule, Max will need to be ready to jump in and help out.

Furthermore, programmers don't want to work in isolation. Perspective on the scope of the entire project engenders professional growth and creates better team spirit and job satisfaction. Max might polish his technical skills by studying Debby's database design because Debby knows much more about databases than Max does.

The project must balance a tightrope. It is valuable for Max to understand the database structure, but harmful for his code to depend on it. Programmers must understand more than they can let their code show. Interfaces and implementation must be a property of software, not of the people who author the software.

THE HIERARCHY OF INTERFACES

Successful implementation and maintenance depend on well-defined interfaces. Part of the job of the design phase is to define interfaces that will allow interchangeability of versions of modules and thereby facilitate configuration management. If the design is not done well (or is not done at all), configuration management becomes a more difficult proposition.

Interfaces themselves are objects to be controlled by the configuration manager. Just like source code and object code, each interface is likely to be revised and varied into multiple versions.

For both of these reasons, interfaces are an important concern of the configuration manager.

Interfaces are created during the design phase of the project. Interfaces are, in fact, the primary output and purpose of the design phase. Design begins with the entire software product viewed as a single entity. Its interfaces are with the outside world and are called the *functional requirements* of the software product. The functional requirements define what the finished software must do.

The first job of the designers is to break down (*decompose*) the software product into a group of modules and to designate the interfaces among the modules. Each module is then designed by being broken into submodules. The process continues recursively until the submodules are so small that their implementation is obvious; then the design is complete.

At each iteration, the designer is faced with the task of deciding how a module of software is going to work. The

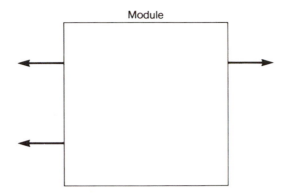

Figure 4.2

designer accomplishes this by specifying the component submodules: what they are, what purpose they serve, and how they interact to accomplish the work of the module. Having identified the submodules, the designer moves on to the next iteration, which is to design the submodules.

The design of a module can be expressed with a picture, as shown in Fig. 4.2. The design begins with a box that represents the module, and outgoing lines that represent the interfaces the module must meet. The box is empty, showing that the implementation is not designed.

The design of the implementation is then expressed with smaller boxes that represent submodules. Lines connecting the smaller boxes represent the interfaces among them (see Fig. 4.3).

As the design process recurses, the submodules are similarly designed, starting with their interfaces and developing their implementation. What is implementation to the designer of the module is interface to the designer of the submodule.

Figure 4.3

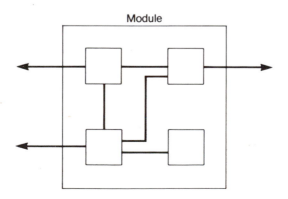

A large software development project must maintain a hierarchy of interfaces that reflects the decomposition of the software. The top level is the functional requirements interface, which specifies what the entire software product must do. The next levels are the interfaces among the modules, followed by the interfaces among the submodules, and so on.

The decomposition of the software into modules and submodules is frequently reflected in the organization of the project into teams and subteams. The eventual level of software decomposition is sufficiently small that the smallest submodule is wholly the responsibility of one person, who is responsible for many such submodules. Typically, the smallest submodule is a subroutine.

By organizing the teams to match the decomposition of software, the interfaces between modules become the interfaces between teams. Each team is then charged with building a single piece of software subject to testable criteria— the interfaces. The team is then a subproject of its own, with its own set of requirements.

PRECISION OF INTERFACES

It is the nature of design not to be a one-pass affair. No real software is designed starting at the very top level, with a strictly recursive decomposition. Real design is done by making tentative decisions and backing up to fix or refine them when necessary. The first time a module is decomposed into submodules, the designer will not be able to define precise interfaces among the submodules, but will know only the approximate responsibilities of the submodules and the approximate nature of the interfaces. Refinement of the interfaces will have to be a matter for negotiation among the subteams responsible for the submodules.

For this reason, an interface is frequently specified in successive degrees of precision as reflected in successive revisions of the interface. The first revision of the interface gives the approximate nature (the purpose) of the interface. Design of the interface is complete when the latest revision is fully precise, sufficient for the coding and maintenance of the participating modules. Further revisions of the interface, prepared during implementation, test, and maintenance, are used to correct errors or make improvements.

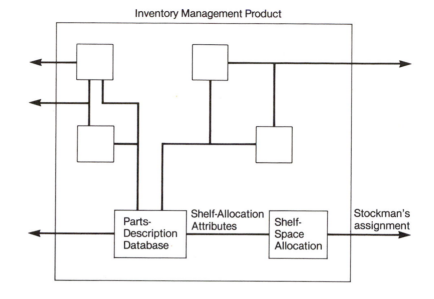

Inventory Management Product

Figure 4.4

Consider Max and Debby's inventory management system project. The designer of the product has specified that two of the submodules are called Shelf-Space Allocation and Parts-Description Database. Max has been assigned to design and implement the former, and Debby has been assigned to the latter. The system designer specified an interface between the two modules called Shelf-Allocation Attributes Interface. The design of the product might look like Fig. 4.4, where only Max's and Debby's modules are shown in detail.

The first revision of the interface, as specified by the product designer, is shown below.

```
          "Shelf-allocation Attributes Interface"

     Participating modules:

          Shelf-space Allocation Module

          Parts-description Database Module:

     The  Parts-description  Database  Module  will  be
     interrogated  by  the  Shelf-space  Allocation  Module
     to  provide  information  about  quantity  in  stock  and
     physical  size  and  weight  of  the  parts.
          Revision 1                      September 28, 1984
```

As Max begins the design of his module, he will decide exactly what information he needs to know about the parts and might negotiate a second revision of the interface with Debby. The second revision is more detailed than the first because Max has developed a better understanding of exactly what information the database must provide:

```
"Shelf-allocation Attributes Interface"

Participating modules:

    Shelf-space Allocation Module

    Parts-description Database Module:

    The Parts-description Database Module will be
interrogated by the Shelf-space Allocation Module
to provide the following information about a given
part:

1.  Quantity currently in stock (in individual
    units);
2.  Maximum projected quantity in stock over next
    30 days(in individual units);
3.  Quantity packaged together (in units per pack-
    age);
4.  Height, depth, and length of a package (in
    inches);
5.  Weight of a package (in ounces); and
6.  Maximum stacking height of packages.
    Revision 2                      October 10, 1984
```

The succeeding revisions describe the exact format of the inquiry, the types and ranges of the data passed in and out, the handling of errors, and further details. In Max and Debby's example, the third revision of the interface is sufficiently detailed for implementation, as shown on the facing page.

TYPES OF INTERFACES

Interfaces among modules come in two basic flavors: *call* interfaces and *data* interfaces.

A call interface allows one module to invoke a subroutine or function within another module. A call interface exists among the module that defines the subroutine (the *callee*)

"Shelf-allocation Attributes Interface"

Participating modules:

Shelf-space Allocation Module

Parts-description Database Module:

The Parts-description Database Module provides the following functions that will be interrogated by the Shelf-space Allocation Module to provide information about a given part:
Function QUANT_IN_STOCK
Arg1: part number; record type PARTNUM; passed by value
Returns: quantity currently in stock (in individual units); integer range 0-32767
Function MAX_QUANT_IN_STOCK
Arg1: part number; record type PARTNUM; passed by value
Returns: maximum projected quantity in stock over next 30 days (in individual units); integer range 0-32767
Function PACKAGE_QUANT
Arg1: part number; record type PARTNUM; passed by value
Returns: quantity packaged together (in units per package); integer range 1-255
Function PACKAGE_SIZE
Arg1: part number; record type PARTNUM; passed by value
Returns: height, width, depth in inches; array (1:3) of integer range 1-48
Function PACKAGE_WEIGHT
Arg1: part number; record type PARTNUM; passed by value
Returns: weight, in ounces; integer range 1-255
Function STACK_HEIGHT
Arg1: part number; record type PARTNUM; passed by value
Returns: maximum stacking height; integer range 1-25
All functions can signal exceptions:
ERROR BAD_PART_NUM -- if part number is not in database.
ERROR DEFUNCT_PART_NUM -- if part number no longer in use.

and the modules that contain calls to the subroutine (the *callers*). The callee provides a service to the caller (for example, a computation or a storage or retrieval of data). The Shelf-allocation Attributes Interface is an example of a call interface.

A call interface designates the *entry points,* which are the names of the subroutines that are provided. For each entry point, the interface describes:

- The parameters, including:
  - □ How many there are and the order in which they appear;
  - □ Type and legal range of values;
  - □ Meanings of special values and end conditions;
  - □ Meaning and purpose of the parameter; and
  - □ Whether the parameter is input-only, output-only, or input–output.

- Side-effects, including:
  - □ Assumed values for global data;
  - □ Modifications to global data;
  - □ Circumstances under which the subroutine might not return normally; and
  - □ The purpose of the subroutine—why it is called, and what it does.

In addition to defining the entry points, the interface might define special data types used to represent parameters (if the programming language permits programmer-defined types).

A *data* interface describes data that is accessed by more than one module. If only one module references data, then the definition is part of the implementation of the module, not part of an interface. A data interface describes shared data, such as global variables, data structures, disk or tape files, or external inputs or outputs. Such an interface is among all the modules that read or write the data.

Included in a data interface is the name, type, and meaning of the data. Record structures are specified field by field, typically using the precise syntax of the programming language to be used. Also described are the time and circumstances under which the data is to be changed, including the initialization.

Max's Shelf-allocation Module shares a file with another module named the Stockman's Assignment Module. The file contains records that list stock that should be moved from one shelf location to another.

```
"Shelf-reallocation File Interface"

Participating modules:

    Shelf-space Allocation Module

    Stockman's Assignment Module


Direct-access File containing 0 or more fixed-
length records.

Records are created and deleted only by the
Shelf-space Allocation Module.
    Field 1: PART; part number of stock to be
        moved; type PART_NUM; initialized at time
        record is created.

    Field 2: OLD_LOC; old shelf location; type
        SHELF_LOC; initialized at time record is
        created.

    Field 3: NEW_LOC; new assigned shelf located;
        type SHELF_LOC; initialized at time record
        is created.

    Field 4: SUCCESS_CODE; error status; legal
        values are NOT_YET_MOVED, MOVE_SUCCESSFUL,
        MOVE_REFUSED, NO_STOCK; initialized to
        NOT_YET_MOVED when record is created;
        modified by Stockman's Assignment.

Revision 3                          October 17, 1984
```

The distinction between data and call interfaces is frequently an artificial one. In modern programming practice, most significant data structures are isolated within modules whose purpose is to provide access to the data for the other modules (as in Debby's case). The physical organization of the database is hidden as part of the implementation of the module and is not part of any interface, so even when a database is shared by a number of modules, the interface is a call interface to a database manager rather than a data interface to a data structure.

THE INTERFACE DOCUMENTS

The interfaces are an essential product of the design phase. Well-defined interfaces allow modules to be coded, tested, integrated, and maintained smoothly, and facilitate configuration management. The purpose of interfaces is to show how modules, built by individual programmers, fit together to form a single programming system. Control of interfaces is a key means by which the configuration manager facilitates communication among programmers. Part of the job of the configuration manager is to make sure that interfaces are well structured, stable, and followed.

So that the interfaces can be followed, they are available to the staff in a public place called the *Interface Book*. The book, which might be hardcopy (paper) or an online directory, is the central library, each entry of which is one interface. Each interface is a signed, dated agreement among project members or teams that describes the interaction between their modules. An interface is a contract detailing terms of cooperation.

The Interface Book is essential to the control of the interfaces. It is written, public, and current. All interfaces are in writing so that there can be no forgetting or conflict of memories. The written interface is current and definitive so that programmers may always refer to it to ascertain exactly what their subroutines are supposed to do. The written interface survives staff turnover and reassignment. Because the interfaces are public, they can serve as the basis for module test.

Interfaces are always signed, never anonymous. The signature certifies that the relevant people have read and agreed to the interface. Each interface is a negotiated agreement. It is essential that all participants understand and are committed to the enforcement of the interface, and agree that it can be met. An interface is never unilaterally dictated, one party upon the other, and is never imposed by an external person not responsible for implementing it. The signature shows a voluntary agreement that the interface is meaningful and meetable.

Interface violations are a central cause of wasted time during integration and system test phases and of regression during maintenance. More project time (and money) will be spent fixing interface violations than on any other single activity. It is inevitable that there will be a multitude of interface violations because an interface for real software is necessarily detailed and complex. English being inherently imprecise, there is no known technique for expressing the semantics of interfaces in an absolutely unambiguous manner. However well the participants believe the interface is stated, there will always be different understandings of its meaning.

To minimize interface violations, each project member has a responsibility to guard against activities that might endanger the interfaces. Participants must not sign an interface they haven't thoroughly read and studied, or that contains details they don't understand. When an interface is found to have errors or ambiguities, project members must never engage in informal verbal clarification. All clarifications must be put in writing as a revision of the interface so that everybody will have the same understanding and so that future generations will understand. Each programmer must continually guard against any deviation between the software and the written, signed interface.

Negotiations to change an interface are commonly initiated by one of the signatories, who suggests the change to facilitate an implementation. Perhaps a programmer can't possibly implement the interface because of the lack of necessary data. Or perhaps the programmer can simplify the implementation, to the betterment of the entire project, by shifting a certain responsibility outside of the module. Max might suggest that Debby keep in the database information describing the frequency with which a part is restocked so that frequently restocked inventory can be placed in a more accessible shelf location. Or he might suggest that package weight be omitted in favor of package density to simplify his calculations. In either event, he must convince Debby of the importance of his changes.

A person who wishes to change an interface will have to endure pressure from other programmers who will need to adapt their implementations to accomodate the change. This will be a powerful inducement to forget about changes that really aren't necessary anyway. The goal is to produce a bias toward stability of the interfaces because no one can successfully build a module if its interfaces are in continual flux. Debby will never get any work done if she is forced to add to the database every new piece of information anybody can think of.

It is a fact of life that interfaces will need to change as errors are uncovered. One of the most common errors is that one of the modules cannot feasibly implement its responsibilities. In that case, there is no choice but to change the interface.

Whenever an interface changes, all modules that participate in the interface must be examined to see if they are still in conformance. The more modules involved, the more people involved, and the more possibility for error. Because interface changes introduce instability in all modules that participate in the interface, it is desirable to have as few modules as possible involved when a change is made. For this reason, the interfaces must be kept very small (on very small topics) so that the effects of changes can be narrowed down to only those modules that absolutely must be involved. Configuration management during coding, testing, and maintenance is significantly easier when the interfaces are small and well structured.

It is far better to have a multitude of small agreements, each on distinct, isolated topics, than to have a few large interfaces that cover everything. In the degenerate case, a single large interface that describes all interrelations between all modules is unacceptable. For example, in Fig. 4.5, there is one all-inclusive interface that tells everything about the interrelationship of Module 1 and Module 2. Even though there are only two signatories to the interface (module 1 and

Figure 4.5

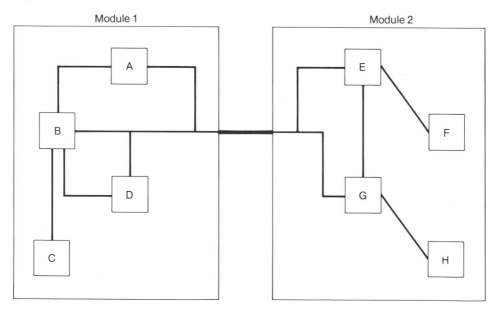

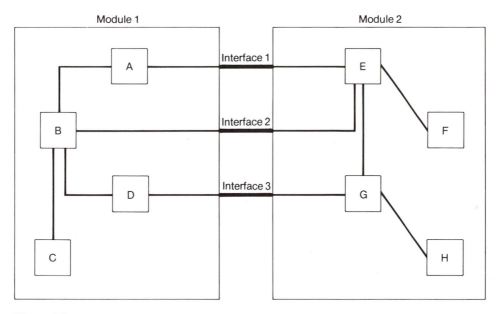

Figure 4.6

module 2), the interface is used by a number of submodules in each module. If this interface is found to have an error, or is for any other reason modified, then submodules A, B, and D in module 1 and submodules E and G in module 2 are potentially affected.

If the interface is broken down into three smaller interfaces, as in Fig. 4.6, then a change to any one of the three affects only one submodule in each module.

A narrow interface provides a limited window into the implementation. The more narrow the interface, the less likely it is to change as implementation and maintenance progress. The more narrow the interface, the fewer the modules and submodules that participate and the less likely the interface is to have errors, to be misunderstood, or to be erroneously implemented.

AUTOMATIC ENFORCEMENT

In the best of all possible worlds, we would want to perform configuration management so that interfaces are automatically enforced. It would then be impossible for programmers to build a module that does not conform with its interfaces. A number of schemes partially accomplish this goal.

A project is to write software in the language C. Data interfaces are contained in a *header file,* which declares the names and types of shared data, including definitions of record types. A programmer writing code that uses the data described in the interface places in the C code an IN-CLUDE directive, which asks a preprocessor to include the header textually into the module prior to compilation. The logical effect is as if the definitions had been coded into the module, but the programmer does not actually write the definitions of the data. Instead the definitions are included by reference to the header.

The header files are protected under control of the configuration manager. Any programmer can include any interface, but nobody can change one without going through a special procedure to secure the approval of project management.

In this scenario, certain aspects of the data interface are automatically enforced. The header specifies the names and types of the data, so the compiler makes sure that all data is used in a manner consistent with its specified type. But there is no enforcement of which modules have read–write access to the data and which only have read-access. More important, this scenario does not perform any enforcement of the meaning of the data.

Consider an alternative enforcement scheme:

A software project working in PL/1 has designed the call interfaces to each of the major subroutines. The interface includes the name and purpose of the subroutine and the types and purposes of the parameters. The project members have decided to enforce the interface by automatically generating as much of the source code for each subroutine as possible, allowing a programmer to code the implementation.

When a call interface for a subroutine is agreed to, the configuration manager generates a *skeleton* of the subroutine source code, as shown in Fig. 4.7. The skeleton is a stub of the subroutine that contains the declaration of the subroutine and its parameters. Comments (delimited in PL/1 by "/*" and "*/") are strategically placed to remind the programmer of the terms of the agreed interface. All local declarations and executable statements are omitted from the skeleton so that the programmer can fill them in as part of the implementation.

```
/*     PROCEDURE CIRCLE    */

CIRCLE: PROCEDURE (RADIUS, CENTER, COLOR);
        /* THIS PROCEDURE DRAWS A CIRCLE ON THE PLOTTER.
           IF CIRCLE WOULD EXTEND OFF THE BED, IT IS
           CLIPPED AT BED EDGES */
        DECLARE    RADIUS        FIXED BINARY (10);
           /* IF RADIUS <=0, NO CIRCLE IS DRAWN */
        DECLARE    CENTER(2)     FIXED BINARY (10);
           /* FIRST ELEMENT IN THE ARRAY IS THE
              X-COORDINATE,
              SECOND IS Y.
              CENTER MAY BE OUTSIDE OF PLOTBED */
        DECLARE    COLOR         FIXED;
           /* VALUES 1 THRU 6 REFER TO THE 6 PEN POSITIONS.
              OTHER VALUES MEAN DRAWN WITH NO PEN */

        /****** INSERT THE IMPLEMENTATION HERE ******/


END CIRCLE;
```

Figure 4.7

The programmers have available a special text editor, which they use to fill in the local declarations, comments, and executable statements that are the implementation of the subroutine. The text editor, however, protects the original skeleton text (the interface) and prohibits its modification. This special text editor lets the programmer freely create and evolve the implementation of the subroutine, but prohibits modification to the declarations of the names and types of the parameters.

In these examples, projects use specialized tools to enforce particular types of interfaces. The C project uses an INCLUDE capability in the C compiler, whereas the PL/1 project develops a special text editor that allows free access to one part of a file (the implementation), and prohibits access to other parts (the interface).

Compilers for modern programming languages are designed to help check for particular kinds of nonconformance to interfaces. It is common for compilers to check subroutine calls to make sure that actual parameters match the types shown in the subroutine definition. Compilers commonly check references to variables to make sure that the type is properly used (for example, that strings are not summed together). Both of these are examples of the compiler checking for conformance to interfaces; the first is a check of a call interface, and the second is a check of a data interface.

On a large programming project, however, the size of the code prohibits presenting all modules simultaneously to the compiler as one compilation. Modules are presented to the compiler independently. Most compilers are not equipped to check for conformance to interfaces among modules that are separately compiled.

In some languages (e.g., FORTRAN), data that is shared among separately compiled modules must be defined in duplicate. A FORTRAN COMMON declaration is written in each module that shares the data. In a language such as this, the configuration manager might describe each data interface by writing a file that contains a COMMON declaration. A programmer writing a module that participates in the interface uses an INCLUDE statement, which directs the compiler's preprocessor to fetch the text of the interface and include it in the module. The compiler then treats the definitions in the COMMON as if they had been coded as part of the module, and performs normal type checking of references against definitions. In FORTRAN, this mechanism is not useful for call interfaces because subroutine definitions cannot appear in COMMON. (This is much the same as the solution in the C example earlier in this section. In C, the header file takes the place of the COMMON declaration and may include definitions of both data and functions, but not the parameters of the functions. The compiler can check for correct use of the types of data and of the return values of functions, but cannot check the types of parameters.)

In the language JOVIAL (used primarily by the U.S. Air Force), the concept of COMMON is advanced to the broader concept of a COMPOOL (COMmon POOL). A COMPOOL can be used to specify either a data or call interface. The COMPOOL contains definitions of types (e.g., records and their fields), data, and subroutines. Subroutine definitions include the names and types of the parameters. A COMPOOL is a single file, typically representing a single interface.

A programmer writing a module that participates in an interface references the appropriate COMPOOL, and the compiler introduces the definitions stored there into the module, similar to FORTRAN preprocessor inclusion. Each JOVIAL module that participates in the interface references the COMPOOL, and the JOVIAL compiler automatically checks the module for conformance to the interface. Unlike FORTRAN COMMON, the JOVIAL COMPOOL mechanism allows the compiler to check conformance to call interfaces as well as data interfaces. For a call interface, the JOVIAL compiler checks both the caller module (that which references the subroutines) as well as the callee (that which defines the implementations of the subroutines) for conformance to the interface.

In both the FORTRAN and JOVIAL examples, the interface file can be protected by the configuration manager so that it is not changed except in a controlled manner. When the interface file is changed, all participating modules must be manually identified and resubmitted to the compiler to verify that they are still in conformance.

The language Ada, recently developed by the U.S. Defense Department, represents further advancement in the area of automatic interface enforcement. Ada is designed for the production of large programs that involve a number of compilation units individually presented to the compiler. Ada checks for conformance to interfaces even when modules are presented separately to the compiler. Interface enforcement is a fundamental design characteristic of Ada.

The major element of program structure in Ada is the *package*, which is a module with a precisely defined interface to the other modules of the program. A package provides data and/or subroutines to the other modules of the program. In Ada, a package's interface is called its *specification* and includes definitions of variables, data types, and calling sequences for subroutines.

An example Ada package specification is shown in Fig. 4.8. This package is used to store a stack of data. The specification includes the definition of the type of data to be stacked, a publicly accessible variable that holds the number of entries currently on the stack, and the definitions of two procedures, called *Push* and *Pop*, each with one parameter. The type definition, variable, and two procedure definitions constitute the complete interface to the package. Note that procedure-calling sequences are defined, but their algorithms (implementation) are not. Lines beginning with two dashes ("--") are comments.

```
Package Manage_Stack is
-- this package provides push/pop services for values of the
-- following type:
    type Stacking_Type is
    record
       Header: character;
       Body: integer range 0 .. 5000;
    end record;

-- the following variable tells how big the stack is:
   Number_on_Stack: integer range 0 .. 32767;
                        --total number of entries on stack

-- the following procedures are used to push and pop:
   procedure Push (New_Value: in Stacking_Type);
                    -- Push the argument onto the stack
   procedure Pop (Old_Value: out Stacking_Type);
                    -- Retrieve top-of-stack

   end Store_Data;
```

Figure 4.8

When another module avails itself of the services of this package (by accessing the variable *Number_on_Stack*, or by calling the procedures, or by declaring a variable of type *Stacking_Type*), the module refers to the package specification and doesn't restate the definitions contained there. The compiler checks for conformance to the interface by making sure that all subroutine calls and definitions match the specified calling sequences and that all variables are referenced in a manner consistent with their defined type.

The Ada compiler checks for conformance to the interface even though the interface (i.e., the package specification) and the module that references the interface are presented in separate compiler invocations. If a module passes incorrect parameters to a subroutine, the compiler refuses to accept the code, even if the specification defining the subroutine was compiled weeks or months earlier.

The implementation of the interface is called the *body* of the package. The body includes the algorithms that implement the subroutines defined in the specification. The package body can be a compilation unit wholly separate from the package specification, thereby enforcing the distinction between interface and implementation. Just as the compiler checks all modules that use an interface, it also checks the module that implements the interface. The compiler checks the body for conformance to the interface to make sure that the implementation strictly obeys the specification provided. A programmer cannot, for example, mistype the definition of a variable, unilaterally decide that an additional argument is necessary for a procedure, or add a new field to a data record.

In Ada, once an interface is agreed to by all parties, it is presented to the compiler, which records it and enforces it against all participants. The Ada compiler is an active participant in the software implementation process, acting as policeman to enforce agreed-upon interfaces and acting as historian to uncover software that needs to be reexamined when an interface is modified. When an interface is changed, the revised package specification is presented to the compiler. The modules that reference the interface, as well as the module that implements the interface, must now be recompiled so that the compiler can check to see if they are still in conformance. Unlike the preceding FORTRAN or JOVIAL examples, in which identification and recompilation of participating modules is a manual process, Ada compilers identify modules that need to be recompiled and refuse to allow unchecked object code to be used. Chapter 8 contains additional discussion of the use of Ada for interface control.

Nobody can pretend that Ada or any other commonly used language provides the complete solution to interface enforcement. An Ada compiler can make sure that the number and type of parameters to a subroutine are correct, that a data object is used in a manner consistent with its type, or that object code is compatible with the most recent revision of interfaces. But no compiler can make sure that the subroutine does the right thing, or that the correct value is stored into the data object at the right time. To make sure that an interface is correctly implemented in its semantics as well as its syntax, testing is necessary. Testing is, of course, the ultimate enforcement of interfaces.

5

C hapter 1 discusses the problems of shared data and simultaneous update. These problems are a significant degradation to the productivity of a programming team. It is inherent in the nature of a team programming project that software needs to be shared among the members of the team. Although well-designed interfaces allow programmers a level of independence, the pieces at some point must be brought together, tested, refined, and maintained as an integrated whole.

Central to the programming team is a database that includes source code, object code, and other components of the eventual product. Because the database is shared among the team, there are conflicts as the programmers try to read and write the same data. There is confusion and mistakes, and each person interferes with the progress of others. Even actions that don't seem to be mistakes can hinder the team progress. This chapter presents techniques for controlling and coordinating access to the shared database in such a way that team productivity is maximized.

Baselines and Private Workspaces

THE IMPORTANCE OF STABILITY

It is not possible to overemphasize the importance of stability to successful software development. Nothing is more frustrating to programmers than not being in control of changes affecting the program they are trying to get working. Consider an example:

> Mark Meticulous has a problem. There is a bug in a module for which he is responsible. It is a serious bug, and the customer is justifiably irate. The system crashes about once a day, and each time the system crashes, it crashes in a different way.
>
> After careful study, Mark has determined that the problem is a corruption in a static data area. Somewhere there is a subscript out of range, an invalid pointer, or

some similar problem that is causing garbage to be placed randomly in the static data area.

The first step in fixing the bug is to make it reproducible, so Mark has spent a week developing an intricate session with the interactive debugger that causes the problem to be dependably reproduced. He has succeeded in causing the error to appear in a particular repeatable way—as a corruption of a specific field in a particular record in static storage. Mark can now begin to find out why that particular field is being corrupted in these circumstances.

Using the debugger and traces, Mark is carefully working backward from the point of corruption, trying to find why the problem happens. Suddenly the bug is no longer repeatable, and that particular field is no longer being corrupted. The system still crashes, but now the nature of the crash is random again. The bug has moved. What happened?

What happened is that someone else modified some other subroutine unrelated to the module Mark was working on. The allocation of code and data is such that everything has been moved to slightly different locations. Now there is something completely different being corrupted, so Mark has to start over again from the beginning and try once again to develop a mechanism for dependably producing the bug.

Mark is justifiably upset. Though the other programmer was just fixing a bug (and fixing it correctly), Mark has lost considerable time, and the customer is still irate. Nobody made a mistake or did anything wrong, but still productivity was lost.

Compare Mark's problem with the example of Bill Barnstormer in Chapter 1. In Bill's case, we were worried that he might introduce defective changes in the software, thereby interfering with the progress of others. But in Mark's situation, we don't care if the change is defective or not. It is the fact that *any* change occurred that destroyed Mark's progress. For Mark, stability is the issue, not mistakes. Mark wants to know that, for a period of time, the shared database of source code will be unchanged.

Mark wants the database of shared source code to be unchanged while he is finding the bug, but he will later need to introduce a fix. Then, he will want to change the shared source code to fix the bug so that he can deliver new software to the customer. For Mark's maximum productivity, he will want complete control of the data—unchanged when he wants it unchanged, and changeable when he wants to make a change.

Unfortunately, this is not a one-person project. All programmers want the database to be stable when they want it to be stable, and changeable when they want to make a change. All programmers want full control, and their maximum productivity depends on it. But the fact that each team member needs both stability and the right to change leads to a conflict. This is the essence of the team coordination problem. Somehow we have to trade off elements of individual productivity to maximize the team productivity.†

If the goal is to prevent conflicting access to a shared database, then one approach would be to give each of the programmers on the team a private copy of the source code database. It would be perfectly stable against outside changes, and the programmer could change it any time. At all times, the programmer could know exactly what is there, have absolute control, and would be working in complete isolation. During the very early stages of implementation, this is the preferred approach. Programmers can build their modules in isolation and test them against their understanding of the interfaces they must meet. Initial implementation, which includes coding and module test, can proceed very quickly because of the ease of working in isolation.

The programmers are working on a single product, so eventually this isolation is unacceptable. The time must come (at the integration testing phase) when programmers must integrate their work with that of the other team members. The good work done by each individual must be propagated to the others so that all can build toward a complete, integrated product. Isolation is unacceptable during integration testing and product maintenance.

If each programmer has a copy of the whole source code, we have a classic double maintenance situation. A program-

---

†It is interesting to note that team productivity is not always the goal. If the customer is sufficiently irate (and sufficiently important), the manager might decide that Mark's productivity in fixing the bug is more important than the team's overall productivity. If everybody else has to take a vacation so that Mark can work without interference, then so be it. This is not, of course, the normal situation.

mer who fixes a bug must transmit the fix to the other programmers, who must make the change in their private
database. The workload will be unacceptable and the databases will diverge. If we have fifteen programmers, each
working in isolation, how can we hope to reconcile the fifteen different databases when the time comes to deliver the
product?

We must devise a mechanism for granting programmers
a measure of control over their own stability and at the same
time allow them to integrate their work with the other team
members to produce a complete product. Programmers will
not be able to be as productive as they could be if they were
working alone, but team productivity will be enhanced.

PRIVATE WORKSPACES

One solution to the team coordination problem is to use a
project *baseline* in conjunction with individual *workspaces*
for each programmer.

The *baseline* is the shared project database. It contains
all the components (source code, object code, etc.) from
which the eventual delivered product will be created. It contains the *library* of modules, as described in Chapter 2. Access to the baseline is sharply restricted—programmers do
not simply go in and change source code if they find a bug.
The contents of the baseline are tightly controlled to ensure
integrity.

Each programmer has a private *workspace*, which can
contain information copied from the baseline. The workspace does not contain all of the project data, but only that
part that its owner chooses to include in it at any given time.
The owner has complete control over its contents and is the
only one who may change anything in it. It is stable when
the owner wants it to be stable, and changeable when a
change must be made.

The private workspace is the place to try out new code.
The baseline is the place to put data that is known to be good.
Included in both workspaces and the baseline might be
source code, object code, load images, documentation, or test
cases.

Figure 5.1 illustrates the baseline and the private workspaces. Each circle represents a *file structure*, which can include source code, object code, or other data. If the

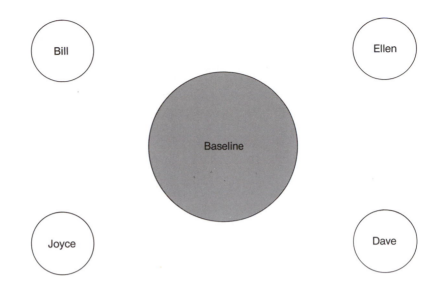

Figure 5.1

programming environment is a directory-oriented operating system (e.g., Unix), the file structure might be a particular directory. In other programming environments, the file structure might be a disk pack, a logical disk volume, or even a cabinet for storage of floppy disks or punch cards. The nature of the storage medium is not fundamental. A file structure is any place in which data can be stored. One file structure is the baseline, and others are for the members of the programming team.

The baseline contains the definitive copy of each module. A programmer who needs to make a change to any module does not change the baseline's copy. Instead, the programmer makes a copy of it from the baseline into the workspace. In Fig. 5.2, Bill has made a copy of the file named A into his workspace. Bill may then freely change this copy in his own workspace.

Bill edits and compiles A in his own workspace, producing a revised version of A. He may change his own copy of A as often as he likes until he is satisfied. To test his revisions, he links his copy of A with baseline copies of other modules he isn't changing to form an executable load image, as shown in Fig. 5.3. Bill may link modules contained in his own workspace and modules from the baseline.

Bill runs tests against this load image. If the tests fail, he can edit his private source code for A, compile, and link

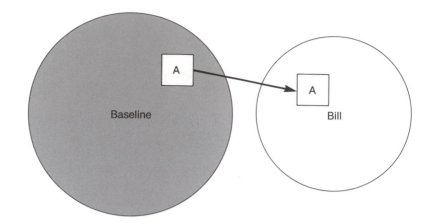

Figure 5.2

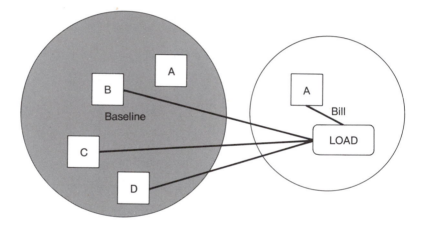

Figure 5.3

again. The process may be repeated until the tests pass, at which point the new revision of A is placed back into the baseline for use in preparation of the eventual delivery and for use by the other team members. After Bill has placed the revised A into the baseline, he can delete his private copy from his workspace.

The fact that Bill can make a private copy of A means that he can check his changes before inflicting them on the rest of the team. The odds are diminished that a defective fix will interfere with the progress of other team members. The fact that there is a public place (the baseline) to put the new revision means Bill has a distribution channel to send the new revised software to the other project members. Both advantages are obtained without having multiple copies of the entire source code database, and therefore without the ensuing double maintenance problem.

LOCKING

We have now solved the problem of Bill Barnstormer, but we haven't yet helped out Dan and Joan, whose problem is presented in Chapter 1 on page 13. Remember that Dan and Joan understood the concept of private databases. Joan copied a set of 20 subroutines from the baseline and will be holding them in her private workspace for over a week before she is finished testing and can return the revised copies to the baseline. Dan, on the other hand, copies one subroutine at a time. He holds it in his workspace for only a few hours because the changes are small and easy to test. By coincidence, there are a few subroutines that both Dan and Joan are working on simultaneously, so when Joan finally returns her 20 revised subroutines, she finds that she has overwritten some fixes that Dan made earlier. A couple of Dan's fixes have been lost. This is called the simultaneous update problem.

Dan and Joan should have adopted a *charge-out* scheme. When Joan copied her 20 routines, she should have arranged for further copying of these routines to be prohibited until she copied the revisions back. Then Dan would not have been permitted to copy the same routines that Joan was already working on until Joan finished.

We need a mechanism to prevent two programmers from simultaneously copying a single module into their workspaces for update. If two people simultaneously update the same module, one of the changes will inevitably be lost.

In an office filing system, when someone borrows a file from a filing cabinet, they leave a manila card that shows the name of the borrower. The file has been removed from the cabinet, so no one else may borrow it until it is returned. This system is not sufficient for the case of programmers copying software from the baseline, however. Although we want only one programmer to copy a given module for update, we would like other programmers to be able to look at the module (with hands off). In Fig. 5.4, Ellen has copied B and C into her workspace for update; at the same time, Bill might want to use the baseline versions in a link so he can

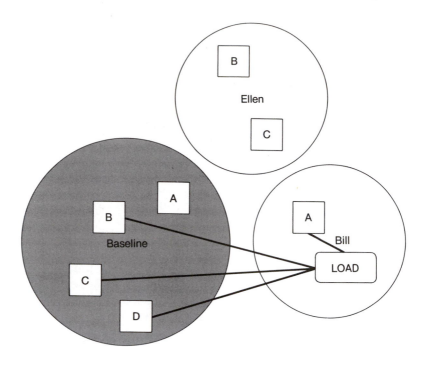

Figure 5.4

test his revisions to A. If Ellen completely removed B and C from the baseline while she updated them, Bill would not be able to use them for his testing. Bill needs read access even while Ellen is updating the files.

It is necessary for all team members to be able to read the baseline copy of a module even while one team member has copied it into a private workspace for update. Though only one person at a time can borrow, all can read.

To avoid the simultaneous update problem, we provide a facility that lets team members copy from the baseline and return a new revision to the baseline. While the borrow is in progress, simultaneous borrows must be prohibited, but all may read. We keep a record of who the borrower is so that no one is permitted to return something that he or she has not borrowed. While a borrow is in progress, read and execute access to the revisions in the baseline is available to everyone.

The facilities for borrowing and returning are called *charge-out* and *charge-in*. The charge-out activity copies a module from the baseline into the programmer's workspace and puts a *lock* on the module so that nobody else may perform a charge-out. The charge-in activity copies the module from the workspace, creating a new revision in the baseline. The charge-in removes the lock so that other programmers may make further revisions.

In Fig. 5.5, Joan has charged-out the module X, and a lock is installed. When Dan tries to charge-out X for simultaneous update, he finds that X is locked. He has to wait.

When Joan charges-in X, a new revision is created in the baseline and the lock is removed (see Fig. 5.6).

Now Dan may charge-out X. Simultaneous update is replaced by *serial update*.

Figure 5.5

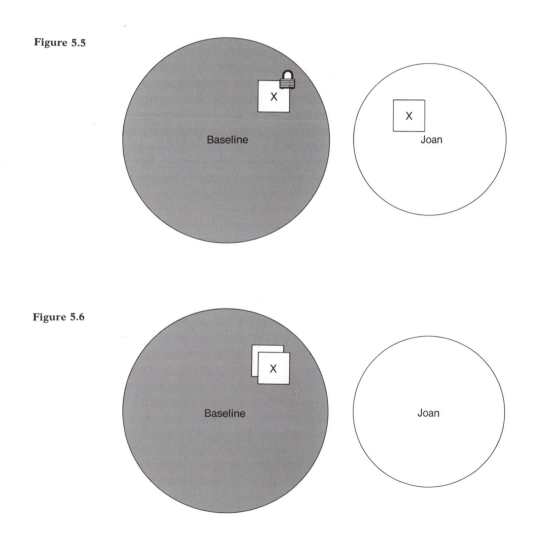

Private workspaces provide a simple yet powerful capability for decreasing the number of defective fixes that become public. It should be clear, however, that the success in eliminating defective fixes hinges upon the degree of testing that is performed in the private workspace. If Bill charges-out a module, modifies it, and charges it in without careful testing, the charge-out/charge-in process accomplishes nothing.

The rigor of charge-out/charge-in facilitates recording of derivations. At the time of a charge-in, the derivation of the new revision may be recorded. This record may include the nature of the change, the reason for the change, the date and time, and the author of the change.

The fact that nobody may change any modules in the baseline except through the charge-out and charge-in protocol means that all revisions in the baseline are permanently frozen at the time they are charged-in. For example, revision 4 may be added (using charge-in), but revision 3 will never be changed. Since no revision in the baseline is ever changed, names of versions of modules are secure and may safely be used in derivations without danger of imprecision.

SHARING

The private workspaces and baseline database are good mechanisms to allow programmers to change shared data with a diminished risk of faulty fixes. With careful use, this system can provide stability.

When programmers want to prepare a load image for execution they do so in a private workspace. They will want to link together modules present in their workspace that they have charged-out and modified. They will also want to link with modules present in the baseline that they have no intention of changing. The process of referencing data from the baseline (for example, so that it may be included in a link) is called *sharing* from the baseline. Programmers must be very careful not to get themselves in trouble with sharing.

Consider the case of Mark Meticulous, who is trying to track down the memory corruption problem that is making his system crash. He is trying to make the bug reproducible, so he copies from the baseline a couple of modules so that he can add tracing statements and memory dumps into the source code. He shares from the baseline the other modules (the ones he doesn't want to change) so that he may complete his link and form a load image for test. He is making headway in finding the bug until one day he makes a new link and finds that the bug has moved because one of the modules he was sharing has changed.

Mark's problem is that he shared module Y. That means that when someone else charged-in a new revision of Y, Mark's next link took the new revision, and Mark's stability was destroyed. A module that Mark was expecting to be unchanged was in fact available to change by another project member. Mark won't make that mistake again.

One solution is for Mark to charge-out every single module that he needs for his link. Although he has no intention of changing these modules, he can use charge-out instead of sharing to lock out changes by other project members. This solution would work, but it means that nobody else can accomplish any work until Mark is finished.

One better solution is for Mark to copy all the modules he needs from the baseline into his workspace. He doesn't charge them out because he has no intention of modifying them to create a new revision, but by copying, he can obtain a single stable version of each module to include in his links. If Mark copies revision 15 of Y into his workspace, then revision 15 is included in every link he performs. Even if another project member performs a charge-out and charge-in of Y (creating revision 16 in the baseline), Mark's stability is ensured because he is always using revision 15 in his testing. Mark is completely shielded from the baseline.

Mark's problem is solved. Though it takes a week to make the bug reproducible and another two weeks to find the bug and fix it, Mark is able to proceed in complete stability, independent of the other project members.

Mark finds the bug and charges out the modules that need to be fixed. Then he conducts rigorous tests to make sure the problem is really gone. When his new system survives without crashing for an entire week, despite his best efforts to make it fail, Mark concludes that the bug is truly fixed. He charges the fixed module into the baseline.

Mark barely has time to plan the celebration before the other project members come banging on his door. Everything has stopped working. The whole world has fallen apart. Mark was not meticulous enough.

What happened to poor Mark, who was trying to be so careful? What happened is that while Mark was tracing down his bug, other people were also working. Dave, another project member, was fixing a bug of his own. Playing by all the rules of configuration management, Dave charged-out module Y, fixed and tested it, and charged-in a new revision, numbered Y(16). The changes worked fine.

Meanwhile, Mark was testing his fix against the old revision, Y(15), even after Dave had created the new one. (Remember that Mark had copied revision Y(15) into his workspace to avoid the instability of sharing.) Mark's bug fix worked with Y(15), but unfortunately did not work with the changes that Dave introduced in Y(16). When Mark charged-in his revision, other programmers used it in conjunction with Y(16), and it failed immediately, as though it hadn't been tested at all.

Mark is in a bind. He *had* to copy specific revisions into his workspace, or he never would have had enough stability to find the bug. By copying instead of sharing, he opened himself up to the problem that actually occurred.

Mark's mistake was that he should have copied the modules when he was looking for his bug and continued to use them when testing to make sure that his fix was correct. But before the charge-in, he should have tested again with the most recent revisions present in the baseline to be sure that his fix was current. After Mark found his bug, currency is the primary issue rather than stability. For maximum security, Mark must make use of both capabilities: copying specific revisions when stability is the concern, and sharing from the baseline when currency is the concern.

INTEGRITY OF THE BASELINE

It is the nature of the baseline that it contains redundant representation of information. That is a classic invitation to a double maintenance problem. We must take measures to ensure the integrity (internal consistency) of the baseline.

An important redundancy in the baseline is that each module is stored as both source code and object code. We want the source code always to match the object code; when the source code for a module is revised, new object code must be prepared. This can be an easy problem to solve: part of the rigor of the charge-in mechanism can be a preparation of new object code for the newly recorded revision.

But the problem can be more insidious and harder to solve. Consider an example:

> A program consists of many FORTRAN modules. There is a central data structure, accessed by seven of the modules. A COMMON declaration, present in each of the modules, is used to describe the data structure.
>
> Henry Hacker, a member of the programming team, performs a charge-out operation to obtain custody of two of the seven modules. As part of a bug fix, Henry finds it necessary to add a new piece of data to the COMMON declaration, so he makes the change in the two modules. The fix works because the new piece of data is added to the end of the COMMON; therefore, the other five modules that don't reference the new data can simply not declare it in their COMMON declarations. Henry tests the fix and performs a charge-in.
>
> The project proceeds smoothly until Tina, another member of the programming team, is adding a new feature to the software. She needs to add a new data item to the central data structure for reference by three modules. She charges-out the three modules (coincidentally, not including the two that Henry modified). Using the same justification that Henry used, she adds her new data item to the end of COMMON in her three modules. The world falls apart. Tina is unaware of what Henry has done, so it takes her a considerable amount of time to realize that her data item overlays Henry's, and is therefore wiped out every time she calls Henry's module.

In this example, the problem is that the charge-in facility could not guarantee the internal consistency of the baseline database because the COMMON declaration is represented in seven places. Integrity of the baseline is endangered because the baseline contains multiple representations of the same information as in the preceding example, in which seven copies of the same COMMON declaration are stored.

Configuration management is easier when the software has an effective distinction between interfaces and implementation. Henry and Tina's problem could be easier to solve if the software had been designed according to the principles of good interface management. The COMMON declaration is a data interface and should be separated from the modules that reference the data. Consider a happier ending to the story:

The configuration manager, aware of the double maintenance problem, knows that it is foolish to try to keep seven copies of the same COMMON declaration in sync. So the baseline database stores only one copy of the COMMON declaration, and a macro facility (INCLUDE) is used to insert the COMMON declaration into each module as part of the compilation process.

Now, if Henry or Tina wants to change a COMMON declaration, they must explicitly perform a charge-out on the declaration itself, make the change, test, and charge-in. The integrity of the baseline is secure because the interface is stored only once.

The interfaces among modules must be separate entities stored in the baseline, subject to their own revision control with charge-out and charge-in. If the interfaces are buried in the implementations of the modules, it is a far harder problem to maintain internal consistency of the baseline.

When an interface is revised with a charge-in, the problem of keeping the baseline's object code current with the source code is more complex than when an implementation is revised. Consider an interface that defines the fields of a record structure. If a new field is added to the record, then the previously existing fields might be reallocated by the compiler. Object code that was prepared with the old revision of the interface will reference incorrect field offsets and will therefore be wrong. Any module that participates in the interface must be recompiled to use the new record structure definition even if it does not use the newly added field.

If an interface is changed, the object code for a participating module might be obsolete even though the module itself has not changed. The charge-in facility must be smart enough to find all the modules that participate in the interface and need to be recompiled. (See the description of Unix *make* in Chapter 8 for an example.)

Effective interface design prevents unnecessary redundancy of information in the baseline. When redundancy is necessary, the charge-in facility can minimize errors. We must be careful to keep the double maintenance monster under control.

We must be careful to keep the double maintenance monster under control.

It is the job of the configuration manager to plan the configuration management strategies for the project. The strategies are implemented using configuration management *procedures*.

The configuration manager gives the designers and programmers the procedures they use to specify interfaces, create new modules, manage private workspaces, charge-out code for modification, and share code with other programmers. Enforcement of these procedures is the means by which the configuration manager helps the software development process.

This chapter discusses alternative implementations of configuration management procedures and highlights problems that might arise.

CASE STUDIES

Configuration management procedures can be either manual or automatic. Manual procedures are those performed by people, whereas automatic procedures require special purpose software tools.

For a small team, manual configuration control procedures can be quite effective. Consider the case of the Data

Tools and Procedures

Base Company (DBC), which markets a database management system.

> The Database Management Support Group consists of four programmers working on functional enhancements and bug fixes. Their shared development machine has on disk an online copy of the source and object code, which serves as the baseline. Also on disk is a file area for each programmer, serving as a private workspace. Everybody has read access to the baseline, including the ability to copy any modules over into his or her private workspace. Once copied from the baseline, modules can be edited. The edited modules are compiled in the private workspace, then linked with the baseline modules for testing.
>
> Only one programmer ever writes anything into the baseline. Her name is Cindy Central, and she is the *project librarian*. Though not a manager, she is the most experienced programmer, having worked with the system for over five years. A programmer who has tested a change and wants to copy it into the baseline gives it to Cindy, who checks it for correctness and examines the test cases that have been run against it. If she approves the change, she inserts the revised module into the baseline.

Before reading further, we should evaluate the pros and cons of this configuration management procedure.

Considering the three basic problems of configuration control, we find that DBC has a very effective solution. The fact that there is only one central baseline means that there is no double maintenance problem. The presence of private workspaces means that programmers can share code without interfering with the stability of others so there is no shared data problem. And Cindy, acting as the funnel into the baseline, eliminates the simultaneous update problem by reconciling conflicting changes.

The group is small enough that Cindy can keep everyone posted about the changes she is making and when she makes them. If a programmer's work demands a temporary stability of certain modules in the baseline, Cindy can hold up changes for a few days until the problem is solved.

The fact that Cindy personally reviews every change decreases the chances that an erroneous or inconsistent fix will find its way into the baseline. Since Cindy personally knows every change that has been made against the baseline, she is in an excellent position to provide advice when mysterious "impossible" regressions occur. Her memory serves as a recording device for derivation histories.

A disadvantage to DBC's configuration control is the indispensability of Cindy. Only she knows what changes have been made. Only she has the scope of knowledge necessary to review proposed changes. And perhaps only she knows how to change the baseline. A manager's most haunting nightmare is an indispensable person.

DBC is using manual configuration management procedures. There are no software tools involved. Though the procedures are human implemented, they are not optional: there is only one way to update the baseline (namely, through Cindy). DBC has a reasonably effective configuration management scheme as long as Cindy is around to implement it.

Manual configuration management procedures need not be centralized through a person. Consider another quite different example:

> The Computer Aided Design (CAD) company keeps the master copy of its software on floppy disks, which are stored in a filing cabinet. When programmers want to modify a module, they go to the filing cabinet and take the proper floppy. They leave behind a charge-out card that gives their name and the date.

The programmers take the floppy to a personal computer and make the modifications, updating the floppy. When they finish, they return the floppy and mark on the charge-out card the nature of the update made.

The single filing cabinet full of floppies implies that there is only one copy of the software, so double maintenance should not be a problem. Only one person at a time can borrow a floppy, so simultaneous update will theoretically not be a problem.

All things considered, however, the CAD company has far weaker configuration management than the DBC has. The procedures are optional in the sense that there is no enforcement mechanism to ensure that the procedures are followed, and there are plenty of opportunities to circumvent them. It's not unreasonable to assume, for example, that often a programmer will forget to complete the charge-out card properly, thereby losing the derivation history explaining what changes were made and why.

Programmers updating a module do so on a personal computer. Because there is no established sharing mechanism for modules not being updated, it is difficult to ensure that programmers are testing the updates against correct copies of the other modules in the system. It can be expected that a large number of defective fixes will find their way into the filing cabinet because of the difficulty of keeping current editions of relevant modules on each programmer's computer.

Quiz

Further critique the CAD configuration control procedures. What shortcuts are likely to be taken that will get the project in trouble?

As shown in the DBC example, manual configuration management procedures can be adequate. But DBC had a team of only four programmers; on a larger project, manual procedures are insufficient. The software is just too large for any single Cindy to be on top of it all. Automatic procedures can make life simpler for everybody. Consider another example:

The Systems Software Company (SSC) is building a large programming system. The staff numbers over 50 programmers. A single online project database of source code and object code is kept, with all project members having read access at all times.

Each project member has a private workspace area on disk. A programmer may develop and test code in a private workspace, then release it into the team baseline.

The baseline is controlled by automated procedures (software tools), implemented in the computer's command language. The operating system access controls are used to prevent any programmer from accessing the baseline except by using these software tools. Tools called *charge-out* and *charge-in* are available to the programmers so that they may copy code from the team baseline into their private workspace. The tools have appropriate access keys so that programmers may update the baseline.

The charge-out and charge-in tools keep a file that records the status of every module in the baseline. For example, the charge-out tool records the name of the person who has borrowed the module, thereby locking the module against simultaneous charge-outs by others. The charge-in tool guarantees that the person doing the charge-in is the same person who did the charge-out. It interrogates the programmer for the nature of the change that was made and keeps a revision history in the log for each module. Access control on the baseline prohibits modification of the baseline in any way except through use of the charge-in tool.

Charge-out and charge-in are special purpose pieces of software provided by the configuration manager to the programming staff. These tools implement a configuration management procedure that requires that programmers may modify only modules that they have copied into their private workspaces. This is an automatic procedure because software tools implement it and enforce it.

The charge-out and charge-in tools are used to prevent simultaneous update. They can protect the baseline against inconsistency.

Since the baseline consists of both source code and object code, it is necessary to prevent the possibility of the source and object diverging. The object code must always be current with the source code. The programmer, who might be forgetful, does not charge-out and charge-in the source and object separately. The programmer manipulates only source code. Charge-out and charge-in copy only source code between the private workspace and the baseline. The charge-in tool automatically compiles each piece of source code that is charged-in, creating its own object code, which is guaranteed to match the source. If the compile fails, the charge-in is aborted.

The charge-in tool guarantees a level of internal consistency in the database, automatically protecting against certain kinds of programmer errors. Other automated procedures are provided by the configuration manager for the benefit of providing a stable test environment:

Each revision of every module is kept in the baseline. The charge-in tool never overwrites a revision of a module, but rather creates new revisions. It automatically freezes each revision so that no revision of a module is ever changed after it is introduced into the baseline. A programmer who wants to test a module in a private workspace may use a tool called *copy,* which provides (on a read-only basis) any revision of any module into a workspace to provide a testing environment.

SSC has the basis of good configuration management procedures. The double maintenance and simultaneous update problems are well under control. When necessary, a programmer can obtain a good degree of temporary stability through the use of copy to provide a testing environment.

If programmers are careful to test thoroughly in their private workspaces before using charge-in, then introduction of erroneous or incomplete fixes into the baseline can be minimized. But, in contrast to the DBC example, there is no Cindy checking the correctness of fixes, so an automatic procedure is instituted.

To check for correctness of new revisions to the software, the charge-in procedure is equipped with a small regression suite. As part of each charge-in, a few significant tests are run against the software using the newly charged-in module. Though the tests are by no means exhaustive, they are sufficient to ensure that the module works on simple cases, thereby preventing gross errors. The results of the tests are automatically compared against expected results, and the newly revised module is rejected if any tests fail.

A more thorough testing is performed every night. In the wee hours of the night, when the computer is normally idle, a large batch of regression tests is submitted against the software currently in the baseline. Actual results are automatically compared against expected results. If any tests fail, notification is sent to the configuration manager first thing in the morning, along with a list of all modules charged-in the previous day.

The automatic freezing of all revisions and the automatic maintenance of revision histories and logs are important steps in the creation of good derivations. Using these capabilities, the configuration manager can record the configuration of every release with confidence that names are unique.

This automatic configuration management is in many ways no more powerful than that supplied by Cindy Central in the DBC example. Because it is automatic, however, it can control a larger project than Cindy ever could. And because it is automatic, there is no indispensable person.

AUTOMATIC VS. MANUAL PROCEDURES

Both manual and automatic procedures can be useful for configuration management. In almost every real-world situation, both manual and automatic procedures exist side by side, with some configuration management procedures automated and some not.

Obtaining compliance with manual procedures can be a major problem because of the possibility of human error (as well as other reasons, which are discussed later). Automated procedures can obtain nearly 100% compliance because use of software access controls can prevent violations. Note that Cindy Central, in the DBC example earlier, relied on the operating system to deny write-permission to the baseline software to the other members of the programming staff.

Manual procedures can, when heavily used, become cumbersome and time-consuming. When the procedures are irritating to use, compliance goes down. In a good development environment, the heavily used procedures are automated for ease of use and to minimize the possibility of error. The rarely used procedures, or procedures requiring judgment calls, can be manual. The greater the team size, the greater the possibility of error in manual procedures, and the greater the number of procedures that must be automated.

It is the job of the configuration manager to design the procedures and see that they are carried out. When sufficient compliance cannot be obtained using manual procedures, the configuration manager must recommend that they be automated.

The decision of what must be automated is not an easy one. The complicating factor is the Universal Complicating Factor (denoted in America by the symbol $). The building of automated configuration management procedures is the building of software, and the building of software costs money, staff, and management attention. For a moderately large project, such as the 50-person development at SSC (discussed earlier), the building and maintenance of automated control procedures can easily consume resources measurable in multiple man-years. It is not hard to imagine that the automated control procedures can be a sufficiently large software development project to require their own automated configuration management procedures (which is enough to give anyone a headache).

Fortunately, it is frequently unnecessary to build automated configuration control procedures from scratch. Commercial packages for change control or source code control are available and might well be sufficient for a small team. For a large team, or one with unusual configuration management needs, a commercial package might provide the underpinnings on top of which specialized refinements can be added. Chapter 7 discusses one example of a commercially available package. Use of a prewritten package can save a lot of money and time.

Even with a commercial package, automated configuration management is not free. When deciding whether to allocate money to automatic configuration management, the project manager must consider the cost of automating against the cost of not automating. The cost of clerical personnel necessary to implement manual procedures is easy to compute, but there are hidden costs. Unfortunately, it is easier to measure the cost of automating than to measure the cost of not automating.

Part of the hidden cost of not automating is the time programmers spend following manual procedures. In the best of all possible worlds, the staff should not have to think of anything except how the software works. The manager would like to relieve them of the responsibility for tracking software and keeping out of the way of other team members. Attention devoted to configuration management is a distraction from the software being built. The decision of when to automate must be based on the cost of automating vs. the lost productivity due to time and distraction spent following manual procedures.

A second part of the hidden cost of not automating is the errors that occur under manual procedures. It is a fact of life that when people use a manual procedure, errors are made. The more people and the more use, the more errors. The decision of when to automate must be based on the cost of automating vs. the cost of the errors when they occur. A presumption of few or no errors is unrealistic.

NONCOMPLIANCE

Noncompliance with configuration management procedures is a problem with both manual and automatic procedures. Automatic procedures can gain higher compliance because they are harder to circumvent.

The first-time manager is usually appalled at the number of configuration management errors that are made. The configuration manager takes great pains to prescribe simple, unambiguous procedures (manual and automatic), but still people cannot follow them. You can explain as many times as you like that each programmer must test changes in a private workspace before charging-in to the baseline, yet every week, the project will lose time and money because somebody didn't. Why is that? Every manual procedure will find people who cannot follow it. Every automated procedure will have loopholes that will be abused or stumbled into almost instantly.

Why is it that configuration management procedures are so hard to enforce? One reason is that it is difficult for staff members to understand the motivation for the procedures. Inexperienced programmers do not have sufficient perspective on the scope of the project to understand how their activities affect others.

To Fred Firstime, adding another parameter to the function he is building is a trivial matter; it won't take the other project members more than a few hours to modify their code for the new calling convention. From the project manager's point of view, however, ten people each modifying an interface once a week means that the whole project is doing nothing but adapting to changes.

As a programmer, Fred sees that the configuration management procedures cost him time and diminish individual productivity; he has tunnel vision and does not see that the group productivity is improved. From Fred's point of view, not being able to add the parameter to his utility means that coding will take three times as long as it should; a couple of hours from a few other staff members can save him two weeks.

The individual programmers see incidents that we might call confusion resulting from a lack of control and think of them as individual isolated mistakes. When one of the other staff members makes a typographical error in adapting to Fred's new calling convention (and wastes a day tracking it down), you can bet that Fred will accept none of the blame. Fred will just see that Joe made a mistake.

Since Fred does not understand the goal (group productivity), he does not truly understand the means toward the goal. He sees the problem only in terms of his own productivity. For an inexperienced project member like Fred, the lack of perspective and understanding makes it hard to remember when to use the manual procedures. When using the automated tools, he doesn't understand the difference between loopholes and intended functionality. It is necessary to teach the inexperienced project members the reasons for the procedures and the importance of following them, both for their personal growth and to ensure compliance.

VOLUNTARY NONCOMPLIANCE

We have seen that one reason configuration management procedures aren't followed is that some people don't appreciate the necessity of following them because they don't understand the goal. There is another reason: the *Renegade*. It is a fact that configuration management is a source of irritation for everybody. The Renegade is going to do something about it.

Some people will challenge the rules: "Why are you wasting my time like this?" These are good people because you can explain to them. Other people will resign themselves to doing what they are told: "I'll do whatever you want. I'm getting paid by the hour." These are okay people because you can put up with them.

Then there are the Renegades. They know that the configuration management procedures (the "bureaucracies") are a waste of time, not to mention an affront to their individuality, creativity, and constitutional rights. They are going to do what they believe is best regardless of what you tell them. They *know* that what they are doing is correct and necessary, even though it violates the configuration management procedures. If they had to obey the rules, they would miss a milestone they have to meet by tomorrow.

> "I can make that change directly in the baseline copy. It's just a one-line edit, so I don't have to fool around with that charge-out and charge-in stuff."
>
> "Changing the source code will take too long. I'll just zap this patch into the object code."
>
> "If I don't change the revision history, nobody will ever know that I made a change."

Renegades are confident that, in the end, management will appreciate what they're doing and will see the error of their ways. They know that when they finish all their software on time and it all works, everybody will understand that they truly knew the best way to get the job done. What is particularly galling is that Renegades probably *will* get their software working on time. It is the rest of the project members who will be late.

BUILDING PROCEDURES

Designing configuration management procedures is an exercise in compromise. You must walk the thin line between chaos and stifling bureaucracy. The procedures must be tight enough that most of the energy of the programming staff is devoted to productive work, and paradoxically must also be loose enough that most of the energy of the programming staff is devoted to productive work. If the procedures are too tight, productive energy is wasted trying to use them. If the procedures are too loose, productive energy is wasted trying to figure out "What program is this?"

A good rule of thumb is not to try to control every conceivable situation. No design can forsee all needs, so allow escapes for manual intervention in unusual circumstances.

The renegade knows that what he is doing is correct and necessary.

Providing procedures for every exceptional circumstance results in procedures that are complicated and difficult to use in the common situations. It is more important that the procedures be easy to use in the common case than that they handle all the esoteric cases. No set of procedures can be powerful enough for all eventualities.

The initial designer of the procedures should attempt to foresee the common configuration management needs and also expect the tools to evolve with time. As pervasive symptoms of confusion appear, new procedures can be developed to address the problem. Better to adapt to real problems than to spend a lot of money and time on a problem that rarely arises.

Modification of the procedures must be carefully measured because stability of the programming environment is essential for productivity. Just as programmers can't work when other people's code is changing out from under them, so they can't work when the programming environment is undergoing continuous "improvement." "Better" procedures are not necessarily better if the increment in quality is offset by the instability caused by modification.

Adaptation and evolution of the configuration management procedures, though inevitable, must be confined to situations of serious confusion. The danger is that the act of introducing new or different procedures will induce a greater confusion than it removes. A perceived inadequacy in the configuration management might be just an exceptional circumstance requiring manual intervention rather than a requirement for new procedures. Remember at all times that the goal is to provide a stable programming environment so that work can get done.

Configuration management is a means, not an end.

THE SAFETY VALVE

Because no configuration management procedures can anticipate every eventuality, it is necessary to build into every automatic procedure an escape valve for human intervention to override the procedures. For example, it might be necessary to allow a programmer to violate a charge-out lock and perform a manually coordinated simultaneous update on a particular module. Or it might be necessary to circumvent automatic regression testing if a test is found to be wrong.

This escape must be entrusted to calm hands. If the escape is used too often, exceptional circumstances will arise out of programmer whim, and control will be lost. Everybody will think he or she is an exception. If the escape is never used, some important work will not be possible.

The escape must never be entrusted to someone who will use it to increase personal productivity at the expense of the project, or that person becomes, by definition, a Renegade. The escape must never be entrusted to anyone who does not heartily support the goals and means of the procedures, or they will undermine them. The escape must be entrusted to someone who is of high enough rank that no pressure can be exerted to grant unwarranted exceptions. The job of enforcing configuration management procedures is not an easy one because of the unpopularity that results from having to deny an exception by saying "No."

From many perspectives, configuration management is difficult. It results in a nontrivial degradation of productivity for each staff member, and each is acutely aware of the degradation, particularly when working on Saturday evenings. Automated procedures require nontrivial amounts of scarce computer resources, slowing down turnaround for everyone. Automated procedures require substantial money to build, consuming that which could be expended elsewhere.

The only way that configuration management procedures can survive these obstacles is if they have the loud-voiced, unequivocal support of management. If management waivers, project members will think they are exceptions, and the procedures will fall apart as each individual tries to maximize personal productivity at the expense of the team.

The degradations in individual productivity can become painful as milestones approach, or as the project becomes late. When a deadline is near, there is a strong temptation to throw the configuration management procedures out the window and make the maximum number of bug fixes possible in a 24-hour day. The result is typically that wrong fixes get made, and the software regresses rather than improves.

Remember that the goal of configuration management is not individual productivity in the short term; the goal is long-term productivity of the team. If the project is running late with good configuration management, think how late it will be without it.

7

The Unix operating system with its associated tool set is rapidly becoming a commercially popular environment for software development. Originally, its use was limited mostly to universities, to which it was distributed free. As university students migrated out into the business world, they have taken Unix with them. Most good hackers cut their eyeteeth on Unix.

Part of the popularity of Unix is due to the large base of university-trained programmers. But Unix also has a number of strong technical advantages. There are three important factors:

1. Portability;
2. Simplicity; and
3. Power.

Portability and simplicity go hand in hand. The fact that Unix provides a limited functionality makes it possible to develop implementations that are easily moved from machine to machine. The Unix kernel and toolset are implemented in C (not machine language) and are therefore easily ported. Though Unix was developed many years ago, it remains today the only commercially significant, multiuser

Configuration Management with Unix

programming environment that is available on a wide range of machines produced by a variety of manufacturers. Portability makes Unix popular because software that runs under Unix on one machine can be made to run on another Unix machine with relatively small effort.

Simplicity and power may seem to be conflicting goals. The fact is that Unix is, by itself, a primitive software development environment, lacking in many of the amenities found in other operating systems. Unix derives its power not through the facilities the operating system provides, but through the wide base of tools that have been developed by users. Unix itself has little power for the software developer, but the Unix user community has built upon the basic Unix building blocks to provide a significant array of software development tools that are available to all Unix users. The Unix philosophy is to provide a few fundamental, primitive functions, sufficient in breadth that creative users can develop (and popularize) whatever power is necessary.

The portability of Unix means that the scope of the user community is not limited to customers of one particular hardware vendor. Because software developed for Unix on one machine can easily be ported to run on any other Unix machine, every new Unix user inherits the full scope of tools developed by the generations of Unix users. It can therefore be said that Unix derives its power, not from functions it provides, but from its portability.

This chapter presents first an overview of the Unix operating system capabilities as relevant for configuration management, then an introduction to two Unix-based tools that provide powerful configuration management capabilities. Finally, there is a discussion of the weaknesses of Unix for configuration management.

OPERATING SYSTEM CAPABILITIES

The important configuration management advantages of Unix include both its management of disk storage and its command language. Each is discussed in turn.

Unix divides its disk storage into *directories*. A directory is a place to keep files, in many ways analogous to a drawer in an office filing cabinet. When a file is created, it is placed into a directory to be organized with files of similar purpose. Users may easily create and delete directories and move files among directories in response to changes in organizational needs. Directories may be nested within other directories, meaning that directories serve to create a hierarchical organization among the files on the disk.

The Unix directory structure is particularly convenient because a directory is a logical rather than physical portion of the disk and therefore does not need to have space preallocated. Files can be dynamically added to or deleted from the directory without worry of exceeding any predetermined limit on available storage space or any maximum number of files in the directory. (In contrast, some other operating systems allow you to create file substructures by allocating a physical piece of the disk; files may be allocated within this substructure only until the available space is used up.) When a Unix file is deleted, its storage space is automatically available for reuse.

Typically, a programming team creates one directory for each programmer's workspace and another for the baseline. Each user typically creates many subdirectories within a directory to organize files for easy retrieval. Similarly, the configuration manager typically creates subdirectories within the baseline.

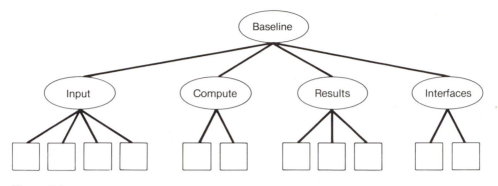

Figure 7.1

In Fig. 7.1, ellipses represent directories and boxes represent files. Lines show the containment of files within directories, and of directories within other directories. This particular example is the baseline of a small programming project in which the software is subdivided by function, with each of the three phases in its own directory. Each module is stored in its own file. Data declarations that are global across the three phases are stored in an interfaces directory.

A typical charge-out protocol might entail copying a file from the baseline directory into a programmer's private directory. A programmer who wants to share a file might use the Unix *linking* facility, which permits a file to be in two directories simultaneously.

An access control scheme is available to enforce configuration management protocols. When users log on to Unix, they must type a secret password to confirm that they are who they claim to be. Once logged on, users may designate certain of their files as accessible only to themselves, other files as accessible to themselves and other members of their team, and the remaining files as accessible to anyone. For each file, users may grant permission to read, permission to write, or (for executable files) permission to invoke. Each file has its own permissions attached, so the owner can grant one type of permission for one file, but different permissions for another file.

The configuration manager, for example, might be the owner of the files in the baseline. The files might include source modules, object code, and executable load images. Some of the executables have undergone thorough testing and have been publicly released, whereas others are under development. Also in the baseline are bug report files.

The manager might protect the files as follows.

User	Group	Other	Files
rw–	*r––*	*–––*	Source and object code
rwx	*r–x*	*–––*	Executables under development
rwx	*r–x*	*––x*	Publicly released executables
rw–	*rw–*	*–w–*	Bug report files

The Unix notation uses the symbol *r* to denote read-permission, *w* to indicate write-permission (to update), and *x* to indicate execution-permission. In this example, the configuration manager grants the team (group) permission to read the source and object code in the baseline, but only the manager (the user) has permission to make changes. The general public (other) is not permitted to read the source and object code. Similarly, the team may read and execute any of the executable files, both those that are public and those that are under development. The public, however, may execute only the files that have been publicly released. The public has permission to write a bug report, but only the team and configuration manager may read the reports.

Other Unix capabilities available for configuration management include timestamps, which are automatically placed on every file to show the time it was created, the last time it was modified (written), and the last time it was read. An important application of timestamps is discussed in the section on the *make* tool later in this chapter.

An important Unix facility available for configuration management is called the *shell*. The shell is a powerful command language that can be used for the quick development of tools. The shell is available in addition to traditional programming languages that can be used to develop more complex (or performance-intensive) configuration management tools.

The purpose of the shell is to allow fast and concise specification of invocation sequences of tools. Using the shell, the configuration manager might build a simple charge-out facility that:

- Invokes the copy program to copy a file from the baseline to the workspace;
- Invokes the change-permission program to change the permissions of the file in the baseline, thereby locking the file against other charge-outs; and
- Invokes a text editor to record the transaction in a log file.

Once the configuration manager has written this charge-out tool using the shell language, team members may invoke the tool when they want to charge-out a file. The three-step protocol, as written by the configuration manager, is automatically performed when the charge-out tool is invoked.

The shell language can be used to combine the basic tools present in Unix quickly to create configuration management tools specific to the needs of the team. The facilities of the shell include macros, variables, loops, conditionals, and other constructs normally found only in programming languages. A facility called a *pipe* is available to channel the output of one program into the input of another (e.g., the output of an automatic interface checker into a compiler).

Unlike traditional programming languages, the fundamental capability of the shell language is the ability to invoke other programs, pass them parameters and input data, and capture their output. The shell language is designed for assembly of basic tools into powerful procedures, and is therefore ideally suited for economical development of configuration management procedures.

BASELINE MANAGEMENT TOOLS

There are two baseline management facilities commonly available for use with Unix. Each is a group of tools that manages a baseline library of source code or other text data files. The Source Code Control System (SCCS) is distributed with most AT&T-derived versions of Unix, and the Revision Control System (RCS) is distributed with Berkeley versions of Unix and independently by Purdue University, where it was developed. Both RCS and SCCS provide the same basic capabilities, although they use different command and option names. Though the two systems are very similar, RCS has some capabilities that SCCS lacks. This section presents an overview of SCCS and highlights the important differences between RCS and SCCS.

The purpose of SCCS is to control the baseline of source code for a software project. (It can also be used to control baselines of documentation, tests, or other textual data.) Each of the files (e.g., source modules) in the baseline may have multiple revisions and multiple variations. SCCS manages all the files and can produce any version of any module on demand. Facilities for charge-out and charge-in are available so that team members may borrow into their work-spaces (i.e., directories) for update.

To minimize wasted disk space, SCCS does not independently store the different versions of a module. Instead, SCCS stores the original version plus the transformations (deltas) necessary to transform each version into the next. For example, if a module is present in three revisions numbered 1.1, 1.2, and 1.3, then SCCS stores the full text of revision 1.1, plus the delta necessary to transform 1.1 into 1.2, plus the delta necessary to transform 1.2 into 1.3. If a programmer asks to see revision 1.3, then SCCS retrieves revision 1.1 and applies the two deltas, thereby producing the complete text of 1.3.

Internal to SCCS, all the versions of a single module are represented in one SCCS file. The file contains the original version of the module plus a record of all the transformations (deltas) that have been applied against the original to obtain each of the revisions and variations. The fact that only deltas, rather than each version, are stored means that SCCS can represent all the versions in a compact form, using relatively little disk space. (It also means that if the one SCCS file is lost, then the original version and all the deltas are gone, so all versions of the module are lost. Backups are critical.)

The SCCS file is named by prefixing *s.* to the name of the module that is being controlled. For example, the original and deltas pertaining to module *output* are described in the SCCS file *s.output.*

Both SCCS and RCS provide commands to perform charge-out and charge-in operations. A programmer who wants to obtain custody of a module that is under SCCS control gives a command such as:

```
get -e s.output
```

This command performs a charge-out operation on the module named *output.* SCCS applies all relevant deltas, and the programmer receives in his or her directory the most recent revision of the module *output.* The option *-e* indicates that the programmer intends to edit the module and later charge-in a new revision; therefore, SCCS locks the module so that no one else may perform a simultaneous update.

The programmer may now edit the version present in the workspace. The programmer, after testing changes, performs a charge-in operation with

```
delta s.output
```

The *delta* command asks the programmer for an English description of the update so that an appropriate derivation history may be recorded (along with the date and other information) in a change log. SCCS creates a new revision of the module named *output* by recording in the *s.* file the changes added by the programmer. A new revision of *output* has now been added to the baseline.

The configuration manager provides SCCS with a user list, showing which individuals or teams are permitted to give *delta* commands. SCCS uses this list to keep unauthorized people from creating new versions.

If a module is only revised (never varied), then the names of the versions proceed in an ascending order (e.g., 1.1, 1.2, 1.3, 2.1, 2.2, 3.1, etc.). SCCS uses a scheme of major and minor version numbers: the major number is the number to the left of the point, and the minor number is the number to the right of the point. Programmers can specify to the *get* command the number of the version they are about to create. Programmers therefore decide when to make the jump to a new major version number. Programmers increment the minor version number when the change is minor and increment the major version number when they feel the change is particularly significant. Other than as a subjective measure of importance, the numbering of a revision as major or minor is insignificant to SCCS. There is no provision for reserving for management the privilege of designating major revisions.

Figure 7.2 is a representation of the versions of a module that is only revised, never varied. The boxes represent versions, and the arrows represent the deltas between versions. SCCS stores in its *s.* file the complete text of the original version 1.1 plus each of the deltas necessary to produce the other versions. SCCS can, on demand, produce any of the versions.

The most common usage of *get* and *delta* is to charge-out the most recent (highest numbered) revision and charge-in a higher numbered revision. SCCS does, however, permit the creation of variations of a module. A programming team, for example, might want to have two variations of a module. One

Figure 7.2

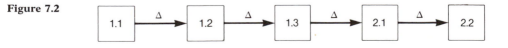

variation includes bug fixes for release to current customers, and another variation includes new features being tested internally for later release. The module undergoes two parallel developments.

The team might use SCCS to designate that version 1.3 is to be varied to form a new version named 1.3.1.1. This new version will contain bug fixes for current customers, as shown in Fig. 7.3.

The divergence of the evolution of the module is called a *fork* in the development. A project might use a forked development to continue to supply bug fixes in support of customers during the period in which a major new release is under internal development. One development path contains the deltas that are the bug fixes, and the other parallel development path contains the deltas that introduce the new features.

To create the forked development path, the programmer will *get* version 1.3, edit and test to add the new functionality, and then use *delta* to create a new version that will be called 1.3.1.1. The first two numbers (1.3) indicate the version from which the new version is derived. The second two numbers (1.1) indicate that this is the first revision of this new variation.

As bugs are fixed in the old functionality, version 1.3.1.1 may be revised as necessary, producing versions named 1.3.1.2, 1.3.1.3, and so on. Similarly, as features are added in the new functionality, new revisions named 1.4, 1.5, and so on, may be created, as shown in Fig. 7.4. The module is undergoing two parallel developments.

The disadvantage of a forked development is the double maintenance problem. A bug in version 1.3 that is fixed in 1.4 might also exist (and need to be fixed) in 1.3.1.1. Duplicate effort is necessary to make sure that every bug fix that is added to the original development path is also added into the development path of the new functionality.

Figure 7.3

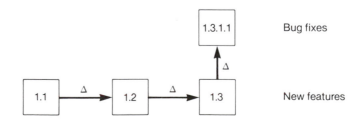

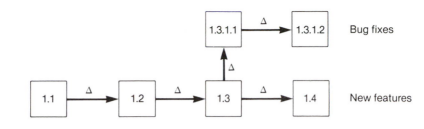

Figure 7.4

One approach to integrating changes from one development path into another is manual double maintenance. When a fix is discovered, a programmer inspects the code in the alternate development path to see whether the same fix needs to be made there. This approach is, of course, error prone and time consuming.

An alternative approach is not to attempt to integrate fixes from one path into the other until the end of divergent development, at which time the two paths are *merged* together. At that time, all the fixes from the original development path are integrated into the new functionality to produce a new combined version, as shown in Fig. 7.5.

Version 2.1 is the new version that contains all of the bug fixes of the original development path as well as the new functionality of the alternate development path.

Under SCCS, the merging of development paths must be done manually. But the RCS system contains a capability for semiautomatically merging development paths. Merging applies all the deltas from one development path to a version in the alternate development path.

Automatic merging of development paths is unfortunately not a fool-proof operation. The RCS automatic merge capability is simply a line-by-line check for differences, in which lines that are changed in one version are similarly

Figure 7.5

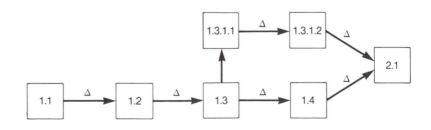

changed in the other. RCS does not make an attempt to understand the nature of the change or what the code is doing, or even to check what part of the line has changed. If the line is in any way different, then RCS adds the new version of the line to the merged path.

It is not hard to devise examples in which the RCS merge becomes confused and either makes mistakes or needs human intervention. As an example, consider the case that a fix applied in the original development path alters code that has been completely rewritten in the new functionality. No automatic tool can be expected to figure out how to integrate the fix into the revised algorithm.

With or without RCS, a development team will not be able to maintain forked development paths and then painlessly merge them. Forked and merged development paths require sophisticated manual analysis, even with the best of configuration management tools.

Naming of versions is a sore point in both SCCS and RCS, although RCS is cleaner. In all the preceding examples, there are only two development paths, and the four-digit numbers are intelligible (though not convenient). But when there are a greater number of variations, the numbering schemes become completely hopeless. SCCS assigns numbers in such a way that the relationship of a number to its position in the development is indeterminate—it is not possible to look at the name of a version and understand how it relates to the other versions. RCS provides a determinate (though complex) numbering system and also allows you to refer to a development path using an English designation. You might, for example, refer to one variation as *development* and the other as *public* so that no one has to memorize the numbers for each.

Neither RCS nor SCCS provides management of object code, load images, or other non ASCII files. The next section describes the *make* tool, which is used in conjunction with RCS or SCCS to make sure that the object code in the baseline matches the source code.

MAKE

One of the most common problems that arises in maintaining consistency of the baseline is guaranteeing the equivalence of source and object modules. A common programmer error is to charge-in new source code and to forget to charge-in matching object code, thereby leaving the baseline in an inconsistent state. The problem is easily solved when the implementation of a module is being charged-in; then, the charge-in procedure can always create new object code to match the source.

But the problem is much harder when an interface is involved. When an interface is changed (for example, a global record-type definition that is referenced in many modules), it may be beyond the programmer's knowledge to know all the different modules that participate in the interface and whose object code therefore is now out-of-date and needs to be recreated. In C, for example, when a header file is changed, all modules that include that header must be recompiled.

One common solution for ensuring this kind of baseline integrity is periodically to rebuild the baseline from source code, heaving out all the object code and building everything again from scratch. On many projects, such a build is performed every night to guarantee baseline integrity for the next morning. This solution, though effective, uses an excessive amount of machine resources rebuilding object code that is, for the most part, not in need of update. The cost of overnight builds can be prohibitive, especially when the software is so large that the build is not finished by morning.

Unix includes a tool, called *make*, that can perform the effect of a complete build without the cost of rebuilding files that are correct to begin with. Make builds a file from component parts, ensuring the currency of all components. It rebuilds only those files that are incorrect, and can therefore be used economically on an overnight basis, or even as a part of every charge-in to guarantee continuous database integrity.

The most common application of make is to build an executable image from a baseline of source and object code. The configuration manager wants to be sure that the executable image reflects the most recent changes to all source code, even if somebody made the mistake of charging-in a new source module and failing to create matching new object code, or of changing an interface and not recompiling all participating modules. It is not sufficient merely to link the existing object code together because some of the existing object code might not match the source.

The configuration manager can use make to prepare the executable image. In the simplest cases, make locates each object module and checks it for currency by comparing the time at which it was last updated against the time the source module was last updated. (Remember that Unix keeps a timestamp for each file, showing the date and time at which it was last modified.) If the source module is more recent than the object code, then the object code is out-of-date, and make will create new object code automatically. Currency is thereby guaranteed.

In the more general cases, simply checking the timestamp of the object and source is not good enough. The object may be out-of-date if any interface referenced by the source code is new, even if the source code itself is not new. To keep object code current in even this more general case, make uses a list of *dependencies* provided by the configuration manager. The dependencies describe the relationships among files. One file is *dependent* on a second if a change to the second might necessitate a change to the first. For example, the object code for routine X (called X.o in Unix jargon) is dependent on the source module for routine X (called X.c) and on any interface files (headers, called .h) included in X.c because a modification to any of these requires preparation of a new X.o.

Dependencies among the baseline files can be expressed in a graph such as the one in Fig. 7.6, in which each file is represented as a box and the dependencies are represented with arrows. The file at the head of the arrow is dependent on the file at the tail. In this example, the executable file *runme* depends on all of the object. The object code a.o depends not just on the source module a.c, but also on an included file incl.h (which contains definitions of global data). Similarly, b.o depends not just on b.c, but also on incl.h.

When the configuration manager invokes make to create the executable file runme, he or she provides a description of these dependencies in a format called a *Makefile*. The Makefile shows that runme depends on a.o, b.o, c.o, and d.o. It also shows, for example, that a.o is dependent on a.c and incl.h.

The dependencies are sufficient to allow make to use timestamps to detect files that are inconsistent and need to be rebuilt. When an inconsistency is discovered, make needs to know how to rebuild the outdated file. This information is also contained in the Makefile. For each file that might be

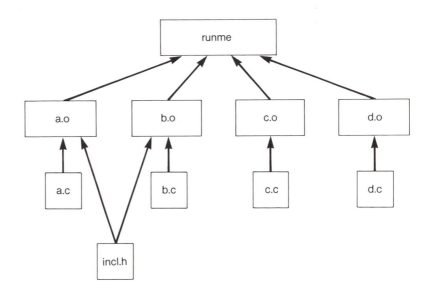

Figure 7.6

out-of-date, the Makefile shows the command(s) to give to create a new one. The command might, for example, be an invocation of a compiler or linker. In addition to showing the dependencies, the Makefile also therefore shows how to *satisfy* each dependency if timestamps reveal a consistency problem.

The following might be the text of the Makefile for the preceding example. (Note that nonstandard Unix compile and link commands are used for clarity of the example for readers who are not accustomed to Unix and the C programming language.)

```
runme : a.o    b.o    c.o    d.o
        linkit  a.o  b.o   c.o   d.o  -o runme
a.o    :   a.c    incl.h
        compile  a.c
b.o    :   b.c    incl.h
        compile  b.c
c.o    :   c.c
        compile  c.c
d.o    :   d.c
        compile  d.c
```

This Makefile expresses the dependence and gives the linker and compiler commands necessary to satisfy the dependencies. A colon (:) indicates that the file named to the left of the colon is dependent on the files named to the right. The following line(s) contains the Unix command(s) necessary to satisfy the dependency. In this example, the first two lines state that runme depends on a.o, b.o, c.o, and d.o. If any of these four files is more recent than runme, a new runme may be created by giving to Unix the command

```
linkit   a.o   b.o   c.o   d.o   o runme
```

Similarly, if a.o is also out-of-date with respect to a.c or incl.h, then a new a.o is created by giving to Unix the command

```
compile   a.c
```

In seeking to make a fully current runme, the make tool starts at the bottom of the dependencies with those files that depend on nothing. Such files are the leaves of the dependency graph. Make checks timestamps upward along all dependency arrows. When an inconsistency is found, it is resolved by giving the specified Unix commands. Files that are already consistent are not recreated. In the most trivial case, it may be that runme is already fully consistent with the source code, and make needs to do nothing.

The Makefile need not enumerate all dependencies. Some are so obvious that make knows about them without being told. For example, make knows that every .o file depends on the matching .c file, and that an out-of-date .o file is created by invoking the compiler. The preceding Makefile could be made shorter by relying on these rules.

The Makefile is created once by the configuration manager at the time the module structure is designed and need not be recreated for each invocation of make. The Makefile needs to be changed only when the module dependency structure is changed—a (relatively) rare occurrence. The Makefile is commonly stored under SCCS or RCS control to facilitate modification.

Use of make is most efficient when the software is designed with a good interface structure, as described in Chapter 4. Interface files (headers) must be small so that changes affect as few modules as possible. Then there will be more interface files, but fewer modules dependent on each. A good module design ensures that *make* rebuilds only those files that really needed to be rebuilt, not files that are unrelated to the changes.

Though make is most commonly used to guarantee consistency of a software baseline, it can also be used to update archives, build documentation, or build software in private workspaces. Make is a general tool for keeping consistency among files and is therefore useful for databases other than software baselines.

UNIX WEAKNESSES

Though Unix has a number of important advantages for a software development team, Unix has a number of significant disadvantages that can be an important drain on team productivity. Some of the Unix disadvantages are unrelated to configuration management issues, but are more general problems related to learning and using the system.

An important strength of Unix is its evolution by contribution from the user community. Creative users over the years have developed new tools that have become standard elements of the Unix toolset. Though these tools are individually well designed and powerful, the total effect is of a programming environment designed by committee. Conceptual integrity and consistency have given way to design by democracy.

Because of these roots, the Unix toolset is difficult to master. There is no standard abbreviation scheme for tool names and no operational standard terminology for passing arguments or specifying options. Invocation sequences are typically cryptic and easy to forget. An option might have different effects when applied to two different tools. For the beginning user, Unix is a series of surprises, each of which must be individually mastered.

Unix was not originally developed to be a commercial software product. Until very recently, there has been no serious corporate support for Unix or its toolset. Most of the tools were developed in a garage-shop environment and distributed within the hacker community. The free-spirit evolution has the advantage that a number of creative and useful tools have been developed. The disadvantage is a lack of support and documentation from developers who are not profit driven. Documentation is typically shoddy and incomplete, leaving to the user's imagination the details of exactly what a particular feature does. Traditionally, the Unix source code is present at every major installation so that if you can't understand the documentation, you can read the implementation to figure out what really happens!

Other weaknesses of Unix are distinctly configuration management issues. A problem that is particularly apparent to the configuration manager is weakness of the access control scheme. More than most other operating systems, Unix is renegade heaven. If an experienced user wants to read a file to which access has been denied, you can be sure that user knows ten different ways to do it—five of them don't even require bringing the system down. Though RCS and SCCS provide additional access controls, any experienced user can easily figure out how to circumvent them.

One classic Unix access-control problem arises when you want to grant the team the privilege to add new files to a directory, but not to modify particular files that you have created there. You will grant write-permission for the directory, but deny write-permission to your files. Then, when team members try to add a new file to the directory, they are permitted to do so, but if they try to modify your protected files, they are denied permission.

If some renegade decides to make "one small change" to a protected file X, all he or she needs to do is delete X and make a new file by the same name! Even though Unix denies permission to modify X, it does permit users to delete it and replace it completely.

It is certainly easy, therefore, to lose valuable information through sabotage (including well-meaning sabotage). It is even easier, though, to lose information by accident. Unlike some other more modern operating systems, revisions are not a concept native to the Unix file structure. Therefore, when you make a change to a file, Unix overwrites the file and loses the earlier state of the file instead of creating a new revision. If your change is defective, you can't get the old version back except possibly from backup tapes. Since there are no revision numbers, files are not frozen by name and artificial mechanisms must be used to ensure the integrity of names referenced in derivations.

Unix provides all its commands with a useful wildcarding facility. Using wildcarding, you can cause a command to operate on a large group of files by using the asterisk character to match arbitrary file names. The command **print***

means to print all files in this directory. Similarly, the command **rm*** means to remove (delete) all files in this directory. Unix lets you delete or modify large numbers of files using wildcarding without asking for confirmation or giving you the chance to change your mind. Every Unix user has a story to tell about the day he or she lost enormous amounts of data by making a foolish typing error.

The Ada Language System (ALS) is a programming environment developed by the U.S. Defense Department as part of its program to introduce the new programming language Ada. The purpose of the ALS is to support programming teams in the development of large-scale software for realtime microprocessor-based applications. The ALS is designed especially for software development in Ada and therefore makes heavy use of Ada's modularity and interface management features.

The software projects for which the ALS is designed are those that typically have severe configuration management problems. These projects consist of moderate-to-large programming teams working on software that will be supported in a number of variations, particularly for alternative hardware configurations. For this reason, the ALS was designed with configuration management as a key design issue.† Support for automatic configuration management tools is deeply ingrained in the ALS design.

Although the ALS was designed to support current state-of-the-art configuration management, the designers realized that the best current technology was still quite primitive,

†The author of this book was the chief designer of the ALS while employed at SofTech, Inc. The reader is therefore warned to take with a grain of salt all discussions of advantages and disadvantages of the ALS.

Configuration Management with the Ada Language System

and that much improvement was necessary and would soon evolve. The ALS was therefore not designed to enforce a particular configuration control strategy that would soon be obsolete. Rather, the goal was more Unix-like—to provide a powerful collection of primitive capabilities upon which any configuration management could comfortably be built. The ALS does not provide a large set of automatic configuration management tools; instead, it provides the building blocks necessary to support sophisticated configuration management tools for the upcoming decades.

The ALS is a valuable case study for the student of configuration management. However, a lack of real-world user experience must qualify the conclusions of any analysis. Nobody, except the developers, has yet used the ALS to build real software.

The newness of the ALS has yet another disadvantage. Like Unix, the ALS will gather power with time. As a user community develops, creative individuals will use the ALS primitives to build new and innovative tools. But this power has not accumulated yet, and the ALS is merely a solid foundation, not a complete workbench.

This chapter presents the basic ALS configuration management building blocks, followed by examples of higher-level tools that are part of the ALS repertoire.

FEATURES OF ADA

Many of the strengths of the Ada Language System derive directly from its support of the Ada language. Ada is controversial for many reasons (not the least of which is its complexity), but the advantages of its support for team software development are undeniable. Perhaps the greatest advantage of the language is its strong support for modularity, interface management, and information hiding. Ada programs are expected to be large and therefore divided into many distinct modules, each separately compiled. Data, types, and subroutines are shared across module boundaries according to well-specified hierarchical interfaces.

A team developing software in Ada typically decomposes the system into many modules called *packages*. Each package is a piece of Ada source code that can be written and compiled separately from the rest of the system. A package is the fundamental construct of information hiding, typically used to represent a data structure and the functions that act upon the data structure. A package can be used to provide subroutine access to a data structure while hiding its representation.

As described in Chapter 4, a team is building an inventory control system. They have now decided to build in Ada to take advantage of Ada's interface management capabilities.

The inventory control system includes an Ada package for the database of suppliers. This package has definitions for all the fields of data in the supplier database. It also contains subroutines that create, delete, and modify records, and functions that conduct inquiries against the database. The database maintains a number of supplier attributes, including name, address, salesman's name, discount schedule, terms, and backlogged orders.

The supplier database package is only one module of the inventory control system. The interface between this module and the rest of the system includes the subroutines that add, delete, or modify attributes of suppliers, as well as functions to make inquiries. The structure of the database, including the allocation, search, and inquiry algorithms, are part of the implementation, not the interface.

Ada allows the programmer building the package to divide the source code into two parts, one representing the interface and the other representing the implementation. The interface is shown in the *package specification,* and the implementation is shown in the *package body.* The package specification and the package body can be two separate files of Ada source code.

Figure 8.1 shows part of the Ada package specification for the supplier database. The complete specification includes the names and parameter types for the subroutines that add to or modify the database and for the functions that perform inquiries against the database. Also included in the package specification are type definitions for the data types that are used for discount codes, supplier priorities, and error conditions. The specification is pub-

Figure 8.1

```
-- SPECIFICATION FOR SUPPLIER_DATA PACKAGE

   package Supplier_Data is

-- this package provides access to supplier database.

-- definitions of data types that are public:
     type Supplier_Code is private;
     type Discount_Code is (All, Never, Negotiated;
     type Supplier_Prior is
          (Preferred, SoleSource, Normal, Unaccepted);
     ...

-- definitions of exceptional error conditions
     Unknown_Supplier_Code:     exception;
     Database_Access_Failure:   exception;
     ...

-- definitions of subroutines that provide access:
     function Make_New_Supplier  (
       Name: in String;
       Phone: in String (1.10)
       ... )
       return Supplier_Code; -- a new supplier code
     function Find_Supplier_Priority (
       Supplier: in Supplier_Code)
       return Supplier_Prior; -- result of the query.
     ...
end Supplier_Data
```

lic to the programming team so that developers of other
modules can access the supplier database.

The Ada package body for the supplier database is of
interest only to the developer of the package. The package
body contains the record definitions representing the logical structure of the database and the algorithms that
manage and retrieve records. The subroutines and functions whose names and parameter lists are shown in the
package specification are fully defined in the package
body, which shows the algorithms and data structures that
make up the implementation.

The Ada language permits the separation of the interface
and the implementation of a package. The interface (specification) is available to programmers of other modules,
whereas the implementation (body) is of interest only to the
developer of the module. If performance considerations dic-
tate that the access method for the supplier database has to
be changed, then the body can be rewritten without changing the specification; hence the implementation can be
changed without disturbing the interface. Ada's package
construct is a direct implementation of the principles of good
interface design, as described in Chapter 4. The Ada language allows (and encourages) programming teams to develop interfaces distinct from implementations.

An important configuration management advantage of
Ada (and therefore of the Ada Language System) is that the
interfaces expressed in package specifications are enforced
by the Ada compiler. If a subroutine and its parameter list
are defined in a package specification, then the compiler requires that every call to the subroutine provide parameters
of the correct type, order, and quantity. The compiler checks
each use of the subroutine against the definition, even though
the modules of the system are all separately compiled. This
checking is not something the programmer must ask for, or
something that requires special *include*-like artificial constructs; the checking is automatic and not circumventable.

Consider the example of a programmer who wants to add
a parameter to a subroutine definition. He or she does so by
editing the appropriate package specification and submit-
ting the revised specification to the Ada compiler. Then the
Ada Language System automatically tells the programmer
which modules participate in the interface. The programmer
can correct them if necessary, then submit each to the compiler for type checking against the revised interface. When

the time comes to make an executable image, the Ada Language System linker refuses to accept object code that has not been checked for conformance against the revised interface. It is not possible to create accidentally a load image in which the subroutine is called with too few arguments, so one source of possible bugs is eliminated.

The Ada Language System enforces conformance to both data and call interfaces. The compiling and linking tools work together to make sure that all modules that participate in an interface are current with the latest revisions of the interface. This sort of cross-module type checking is uncommon in popular programming languages and is particularly useful for ensuring integrity of the project baseline.

The Ada compiler also facilitates configuration management by enforcing the distinction between interface and implementation. The data definitions and algorithms contained in the package body are part of the implementation of the module and cannot be referenced by any other modules. In the preceding inventory management example, note that the definition of the records in the supplier database is present in the body, not the specification, and is therefore unavailable to other modules.

When implementing a package body, programmers write algorithms for the subroutines that are promised by the interface. But, in addition, they might define data structures, record types, and subroutines that are intended for use only within the package. They are part of the implementation. For example, the author of the supplier database package body will write subroutines that perform implementation-dependent search, allocation, and deallocation of records. There will be pointers to record chains and definitions of hash tables. Since these details are implementation-dependent (and might need to be rewritten if the structure of the database is revised), the subroutines are intended to be called only from within the package. These subroutines, then, are defined only in the package body and not in the package specification.

Ada protects the privacy of the implementation. The data, types, and subroutines that are part of the implementation are available only within the module and are not available to other modules. No other module can circumvent the agreed interface to examine the fields in the supplier database directly, for example, because no other module can satisfy the name-scoping rules necessary to reference data definitions contained in the package body. The only access to the database is through the subroutines and functions defined in the package specification. Even if the author of another module should happen to know the names internal to a package, the language does not permit the author to write code that makes use of the knowledge. Using the example of Chapter 4, Max can help Debby write and maintain the database manager (and therefore he will understand its implementation), but the shelf-allocation software that he is building will still be well behaved in its own access to the database through the published interface.

ALS FILE STRUCTURE

The purpose of the ALS file structure is like that of any other programming environment. The file structure is where the staff stores project information such as source and object code, documentation, schedules, tools, and football-pool results. But the similarity ends there. The organization and features of the ALS file structure provide a powerful mechanism for the implementation of automatic configuration management tools.

Like Unix and many other operating systems, ALS files are organized into *directories,* which are subdivisions of the disk storage. Like Unix, these directories are logical rather than physical subdivisions, so they may expand and contract in size dynamically to accommodate as many files as necessary. Typically, each programmer has a directory that serves as a private workspace. One or more other directories hold the baseline.

The other aspects of the ALS file structure are distinctly unlike Unix. Each ALS file may be present in alternative versions, including both revisions and variations. Figure 8.2 shows a directory that holds multiple revisions of a file X. The revisions are named X(1), X(2), and so on, indicating their ordering. In this example, the most recent revision of X is X(4).

Revisions are stored as distinct files, not as deltas from an original version. This has the disadvantage that more disk space is necessary to store the complete set of revisions. The advantage is that there is greater protection against inadvertent deletion of the entire set because accidental destruction of one revision doesn't mean that other revisions are lost. Independent storage of revisions also facilitates tape archiving of older revisions so that disk space is not consumed unnecessarily.

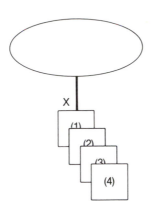

Figure 8.2

Integrity of file names is an essential element of derivation recording. For this reason, the ALS imposes the concept of *freezing* on all revisions other than the most recent. Once a revision X(2) is created, the contents of X(1) are permanently frozen and may never be modified. This means that when a derivation references a particular revision of a file, there is no chance that the revision has been modified since the derivation was recorded. Freezing means that the integrity of the name X(1) is secure.

ALS files can also be represented in alternative variations. Figure 8.3 shows a directory that contains two variations of the file Y. The hexagon represents a grouping of the files beneath into a *variation set*. In this case, the two variations of Y are called Y(Test) and Y(Production). Note that Y(Test) has a number of revisions.

Figure 8.3

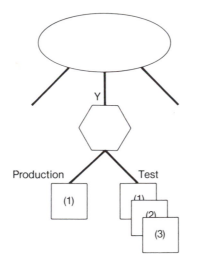

ADDITIONAL FEATURES OF THE FILE STRUCTURE

A person who wants to do only simple things with the ALS can take advantage of this simple hierarchical organization of files (and their versions) into directories. The more advanced user, such as a configuration manager, has available a more powerful superset of this organization of files.

Each file has associated with it properties called *attributes* and *associations*. Attributes are used to provide descriptive information about a file, such as its creation date and its purpose. Certain attributes are automatically recorded by the ALS (e.g., creation date), whereas others can be added by configuration management tools. For example, attributes of a source module file in the baseline might be the person who has performed a charge-out, the date the module was last tested, or the purpose of the module. The configuration manager may define new file attributes as necessary to implement procedures.

Associations, like attributes, are properties of files. Associations are used to show relationships among files. One file that contains a subroutine, for example, might point to all the other files that call the subroutine, or a source module in the baseline might point to files that contain tests that exercise the module, as shown in Fig. 8.4. The arrows represent an association from each module to all its relevant tests. The ALS file structure may contain many associations, each describing a different type of relationship among files.

Figure 8.4

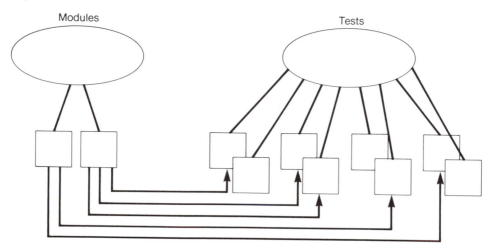

The presence of attributes and associations means that the file structure has all the characteristics of a full network database. Each file can be thought of as a record in the project database. One field of the record is what we ordinarily think of as the contents of the file. Other fields are the attributes. The files are connected in arbitrarily complex relationships, as indicated by the associations. Both new fields (attributes) and new relationships (associations) may be dynamically created by any user (in particular, by the configuration manager).

Attributes and associations are important elements in the flexibility of the ALS to accomodate new configuration management schemes. One particular use of attributes and associates is to record derivation histories. When the ALS creates a file, it automatically records a history, including date, person, tool, arguments, and input files, so each file contains an attribute showing the name of the tool that created the file, the arguments it received, and the reason for creation. An association is used to point to all the files that were used as input to the tool when the file was created. To guarantee reproducibility, files mentioned in a derivation are automatically frozen against deletion or modification.

ARCHIVING

Configuration management tools typically require that large amounts of data be retained, although they are seldom referenced. To conserve disk space, the ALS provides an archiving facility to store seldom-used files on tape. The advantage of the ALS archiving facility compared to more traditional backups is that each ALS file maintains its place in the directory structure (and therefore keeps its name) even after it has been written to tape. An archived file is still a member of the file structure in that it still participates in the relationships shown by associations and the directory structure. The online disk storage keeps a marker for the archived file, including the name of the tape where the file contents are stored. Files can still be read as if they were online (except that access time is, of course, much slower because of the need for an operator to mount a tape).

In Fig. 8.5, the file Z(1) has been archived to tape. It still exists in the file structure, it may be referenced and read, but it is stored on tape instead of on disk, and access time is much slower. The file Z(2) is online.

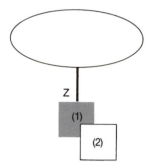

Figure 8.5

One application of the archive is to store offline files that are necessary for the possible reproduction of important data. A derivation can refer to files that are not present on disk (and therefore don't consume storage) but still can be easily found in case they are needed to reproduce data.

ACCESS CONTROL

An important requirement for any automatic configuration management protocol is access control. The configuration manager must have the power to prevent unauthorized people from reading or modifying certain data in the file structure.

The ALS provides a particularly sophisticated access control scheme. Each file or directory has locks that name particular people who are allowed to read, overwrite, add to, or (in the case of programs) execute the data in the file. People can be named individually or can be granted permission on a team basis.

Even this detailed access control is not powerful enough for thorough security of configuration management procedures. Access control based on individual permissions assumes that the users can be divided into two groups: trusted and untrusted. The trusted are allowed the access, whereas the untrusted are not. Such access control is ineffective in preventing accidentally wrong updates by trusted people.

A particular project has instituted a bug-tracking scheme that records each bug in its own file. When a bug is fixed, a description of the solution is placed in the file, and an association is set up to link the bug to all of the source modules that were changed to make the fix. Furthermore, each revised source module has an association pointing back to the bug to show why the revision was made. Figure 8.6 shows an example of the relationships between a fixed bug and the two source modules that were revised to implement the fix.

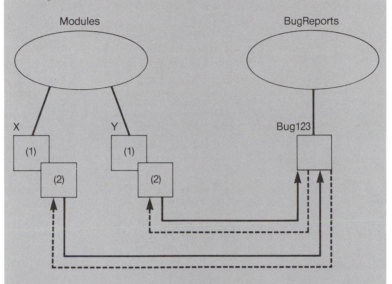

Figure 8.6

For each revision of a module, the association drawn in solid lines shows which bug report prompted the fix. The association drawn in dashed lines shows which modules were fixed to correct the bug.

Any member of the programming team is authorized to fix a bug. This means that any member must be authorized to write information into each bug report and to set up the associations between the bug report and the source modules.

The process of recording a bug fix has a number of steps, and the configuration manager does not want to take the chance that a programmer might accidentally set up the associations incorrectly, causing a bug report to be lost. The configuration manager therefore wants to create a special bug report tool that automatically records all the attributes and associations. All programmers will be required to use this tool when they record a bug fix; they will not be permitted to record the fix manually.

The ALS provides the configuration manager with a convenient access control mechanism for implementing a plan. Any file can be protected with two kinds of locks: one lock restricts the people who may access; the other lock restricts the tools they may use. In the preceding example, each bug report would be protected with locks that would grant the entire programming staff write-permission, but only if they use the bug report tool to do so. Nobody (not even an authorized person) may use a simple text editor to add a description of the solution or use a simple create-association tool to create the association link to the revised source modules. Although the programmers are trusted with judgment, only the bug report tool is trusted not to make mistakes.

Access control specifies both the people who may access and the tools that may be used for access. Figure 8.7 shows that each bug report file is protected with two kinds of locks and that two kinds of keys are required to gain access. One lock specifies the people who may write. The other lock specifies the tool and is called the *via* lock. An authorized person is granted access only via authorized tools. Both locks must be opened before the file may be accessed. In the example, the file may be modified only by an authorized person (i.e., a member of the programming team) using an authorized tool (i.e., the bug report tool).

Figure 8.7

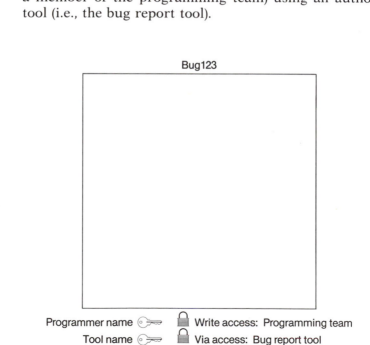

Bug123

Programmer name ⚷   Write access: Programming team
Tool name ⚷   Via access: Bug report tool

The configuration manager might use the via lock when integrity of data requires that multiple consistent changes be made in the file structure. When one change demands another (or else the data is inconsistent), the configuration manager creates a tool that ensures that all changes are made at once. The data is protected against access other than via this trusted tool, thereby preventing mistakes and eliminating what would otherwise be a data integrity problem.

The ALS uses via control to protect object code. All object code is stored in a special kind of directory called a *program library*. The Ada compiler and linker use attributes and associations among the object code to implement the cross-module type checking that is fundamental to Ada interface management. Program libraries are protected with the via attribute to make sure that the attributes and associations are correctly maintained and to ensure that Ada can correctly enforce interfaces.

9

Now it is time to apply the principles of configuration management. This chapter discusses, in concrete terms, the role of the configuration manager throughout a sample software project and suggests some specific solutions to configuration management problems.

Projects differ in many respects, including availability of hardware and software tools, size and expertise of team, type of software being built, and programming language being used. For these and many other reasons, it is not possible to describe a single configuration management scheme that is applicable across the board to all projects. The purpose of this chapter is to suggest ideas that can be adopted or adapted as necessary by a configuration manager for the needs of his project. There is no claim that the solutions presented here are the *only* correct way to do things.

The procedures described here are largely automatic, reflecting a significant investment in the creation of configuration management tools. They are, however, relatively straightforward in intent and construction, forgoing more elaborate and comprehensive solutions that would require specialized expertise or enormous resources. These procedures are ambitious, but are also realistic and feasible for projects of moderate size. For the most part, the procedures described here are similar in scope to those built for a 50-

Applying the Principles

person project in which the author was involved. In that project, the procedures were built and maintained by a staff of three that was dedicated for the duration of the project.

Each phase in the project life cycle presents its own challenges to the configuration manager, so each phase is discussed in turn. The discussion of each phase presents first the configuration manager's goals, then the strategy, then a list of the specific tools and procedures that must be provided to implement the strategy. This sample project builds its software in C, so the discussion takes advantage of features of that language.

THE SYSTEM DESIGN PHASE

The system design phase of the project is not when programmers are thinking about configuration management. The team is typically small and experienced, and can easily coordinate on an informal basis. No code is being written, no bugs are being fixed, and no confusion is evident. To the configuration manager, however, this is the opportunity to introduce control and technique into the development process and to head off problems that would appear in later phases. Now is the time to lay the groundwork for successful coding, testing, delivery, and maintenance.

Goals   The configuration manager has two fundamental goals during the design phase:

- To ensure that the design is structured for maximum modularity and information hiding to simplify configuration management during the later phases; and

- To institute effective change control on the design documents themselves, helping the designers ensure that the documents are current and correct.

Strategy   In this sample project, the configuration manager takes the approach of building a comprehensive database (called the *project baseline*) to represent the structure of the software. The elements in this database are the software components and the interfaces among them. This database is gradually built during the design and coding phases and serves as the central structure for configuration management throughout the project. All the documentation and the program code are stored in or derived from this database.

The first design task is to create the information for the initial draft of the system design document. This document shows the decomposition of the system into modules and the corresponding enumeration of interfaces among the modules. The system design document contains three sections:

- A decomposition illustration showing the modules and their interfaces;
- A description of the purpose of each module; and
- A description of each interface.

The decomposition illustration uses the box-and-arrow approach described in Chapter 4. The illustration shows the top-level breakdown of the system into modules, and names the interfaces among the modules. In the illustration, each module is represented by a box and each interface by a labelled arrow. An example is shown in Fig. 9.1.

The decomposition illustration is an important project reference and is given a position of prominence for ease of access by all project members. It may, for example, be posted on the wall in a central location or conference room.

The descriptions for all modules and for each interface is stored online in the project baseline. Project members are

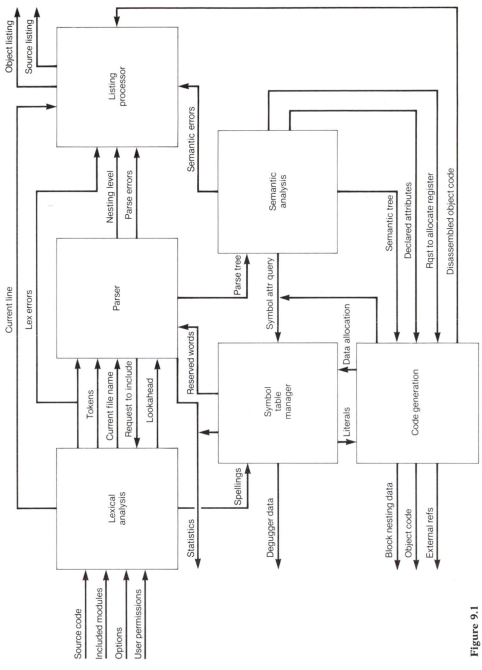

Figure 9.1

granted read access so they may look at any part of the design at any time. The project baseline is protected against write access by project members and controlled with charge-in and charge-out tools. A designer who wants to revise a description performs a charge-out operation, makes the change, and charges the revision back in.

Each description is stored independently in the baseline, so there is one file for each module description and one for each interface description. This independence allows a designer to charge-out and modify pieces of the documents at a small granularity. Each baseline file stores all revisions of a description, representing them by the original description and a series of deltas that describe the changes that have been made to produce the revisions.

A change log is kept for each module or interface description, and every charge-in is accompanied by an entry into the change log telling who made the change and why. The charge-in tool prompts the designer to provide the change log information, and it automatically records it. Change bars are automatically inserted, allowing readers to spot differences between revisions instantly.

The system design document is derived from the project baseline. When it comes time to produce an edition of the system design document, the document is assembled from the most recent revisions of each description in the database. The pieces are collated and numbered into a finished product. The system design document is not static, written once and then ignored; instead, it is continuously improved and corrected throughout the project. The first edition of the system design document contains early revisions of the module and interface descriptions. As design develops, the descriptions stored in the project baseline (and, therefore, appearing in later editions of the system design document) become more precise and more accurate.

To ensure that all the descriptions contain complete information represented in a consistent manner, the configuration manager controls the format of each description. A designer who wants to describe an interface or module does so by answering questions. Figure 9.2 shows an example of the questions that are answered to describe a module. The designer answers the questions shown, and a description of the module is automatically prepared in the correct format for inclusion in the baseline database, and eventually in the system design document.

```
                        MODULE DEFINITION

   MODULE NAME: _ _ _ _ _ _ _ _ _ _ _ _ _ _
   Purpose: _____
   _____
   _____

   Implementation language: C __; Macro __; FORTRAN __.
   Privilege: User __; Supervisor __; Kernel __.
   Permanence: Paged __; Resident __; ROM __.
   Algorithm: _____
   _____
   _____
   _____

   Provides interfaces:
            _____     _____

   Uses interfaces:
            _____     _____
            _____     _____
            _____     _____

   Hardware requirements _____
   Porting considerations _____
   _____

   Debugging/Testing aids: _____
   _____

   Errors diagnosed:
            _____     _____

   Abnormal terminations:
            _____     _____
```

Figure 9.2   Designer: _____ Date: _____

Implementation   To accomplish this strategy for the system design phase, the configuration manager provides the following for the members of the design team:

- A write-protected project baseline database containing, for each module or interface, a description file representing all the revisions of its description;

- A procedure that allows a designer to read any interface or module in the project baseline;

- Private workspaces for each designer, in which the designer can edit charged-out descriptions;

- A procedure that allows a designer to describe a new module or a new interface by answering a prescribed set of questions (or filling in a form) describing the module, and that then creates a new description file of the proper format;

- A charge-out procedure that allows a designer to obtain a copy of a description in a private workspace, and which records who performed the charge-out and locks the description against simultaneous charge-out;

- A charge-in procedure that checks to make sure the same person who charged-out is charging-in, then checks the revision to make sure correct format has been preserved, and enters a new revision of a description into the baseline, creates a change log, creates revision bars in the new revision, and removes the lock; if an interface is being charged-in, obtains permission from representatives of participating modules before recording the revision;

- A procedure that records that a module or interface is defunct and no longer exists;

- A procedure that goes through the baseline and collects all the module and interface descriptions and collates and formats them into a system design document;

- A procedure that checks the module descriptions against the interface descriptions to make sure that the baseline is consistent in its description of which modules participate in which interfaces; and

- A manual procedure for checking the decomposition illustration against the descriptions present in the baseline, for example, to make sure that all modules and interfaces present in one are present in the other.

THE DETAILED DESIGN PHASE

The purpose of detailed design is to describe the implementation of each module by decomposing each module into a set of *packages*. For this project, the term *module* refers to the top-level decomposition of the software. The term *package* refers to the second-level decomposition, which is a single compilation unit. Each module is composed of one or more packages. Each package is a single file of source code containing a number of related subroutines and data definitions.

The product of this phase is a description of the packages that comprise each module. For each package, the subroutines and major data structures are enumerated and defined.

Goals   The goals during detailed design are much the same as the goals during system design:

■ To ensure that the design is structured for maximum modularity and information hiding; and

■ To institute effective change control on the design documents themselves.

An additional goal is to organize the baseline to avoid double maintenance for the code and design documents to minimize divergence between the code and the detailed design for the duration of the project.

Strategy   The configuration management strategy for the detailed design phase is similar to that of the system design phase: A designer decomposing a module creates a decomposition illustration showing the packages of which the module is composed. Each package is then described to specify:

■ Subroutines in the package. Those that may be called from outside the package are *global subroutines*, which are part of the package interface to the other packages and modules of the system; and

■ Major data definitions in the package. Those that may be referenced from outside the package are *global data structures*, which are also part of the package interface.

The description of the package includes precise definitions of the subroutines and data structures, defined using the programming language adopted by the project. A designer describing a package completes an online interactive questionnaire, such as shown in Fig. 9.3.

After the designer answers the questions in the questionnaire, the procedure uses the answers to prepare a *skeleton* of the package. The skeleton is an outline of the source code for a compilation unit, containing as much of the package as can be inferred from the information supplied by the designer. The skeleton is the first revision of the source code for the package and is placed into the project baseline.

```
                    PACKAGE DEFINITION

Package name _ _ _ _ _ _ _ _ _ _ _ _ _ _ _ _ _ _
Part of module _ _ _ _ _ _ _ _ _ _ _ _ _ _ _ _ _
Purpose: _____
_____

Does this package provide a module interface? _____
      Which one? _____
Participates in interfaces:
      _____        _____
      _____        _____

First Data Structure:
      Usage: Local ___; Global read-only ___;
             Global read-write ___;
      Name _____
      Purpose: _____
      Allocation: Static ___; Automatic ___; File ___;
      Type definition: _____
      _____
      Initialization: _____
Second Data Structure:
                              .  .  .
First Subroutine:
      Name _____
      Usage: Local ___; Global ___;
      Purpose _____
      Side effects: _____
      Assumptions: _____
      Parameter definitions:
             Parm 1. Name: _____
             Input ___; In/Out ___; Output ___;
             Type: _____
             Purpose: _____
             Default value: _____
             Parm 2.  .  .  .
                   .  .  .
      Abnormal exits: _____
      Errors diagnosed:
             _____        _____
             _____        _____

Second Subroutine:
      Name _____
      Usage: Local ___; Global ___;
      Purpose _____
      Side effects: _____
         .   .   .
```

Figure 9.3

A sample skeleton is shown in Fig. 9.4, using the C programming language. (For brevity, the last few subroutine definitions are omitted from the figure.) Note that the C language uses the character sequences "/*" and "*/" to introduce and terminate comments, so most of what appears in

```
/ ***********************************************************
                    PACKAGE buildstack

                  in module rgcontrol

REVISION HISTORY:
   6/27/85   Skeleton automatically generated from
             questionnaire


PURPOSE:
     This package contains routines that control the master
stack. Routines are provided to initialize, push, pop, and
interrogate statistics concerning the stack.      */

/*
INTERFACES:        */
#include "rectype.h"

/*
DATA STRUCTURES: */

    /* Data structure  masterstack */
    /* Purpose: This structure is the master control stack*/
    /* Usage: For local use only */

       struct rectype masterstack [255];

    /* Data structure stackpoint */
    /* Purpose: This is the pointer to next available entry*/
    /* Usage: For local use only */

       int stackpoint = 0;

/*
SUBROUTINES: */

    /* Function initstack */
    /* Usage: global subroutine */
    /* Purpose: This subroutine clears the stack */
    /* Side effects: All descriptors on stack are cleanly
       terminated and relevant control blocks deallocated */
    /* Assumptions: Stack contains only valid, active
       descriptors */
    /* Abnormal exits: to System Diagnosis if stack contains
       invalid entries */
    /* Errors diagnosed: Code 1 if stack has less than zero
       entries */
    /* Definiton: */

int initstack () /* returns error code value*/
{
     /**** ALGORITHM GOES HERE ****/
     return(0);
}


        .  .  .
```

Figure 9.4

the skeleton are comments. The skeleton is a complete compilation unit in the C language, even though the algorithms of all the subroutines are omitted. (The subroutines are only stubs.) The reader should compare the sample skeleton against the Package Definition questionnaire shown in Fig. 9.3 to understand how the skeleton is automatically derived from the information contained in the package description.

When first designing a package, the designer may be unable to answer most of the questions in the questionnaire. The first revision of a package skeleton might contain only the name of the package, a brief statement of its purpose, and the names of some of its global subroutines and global data structures. Later revisions gradually add more information until the description is complete. The complete package skeleton contains exact definitions of all the data structures and the calling sequences of all the subroutines that provide the package interface and implementation.

During the detailed design phase, the only description of the package present in the baseline is the skeleton, which is source code. Because there is no separate design description, there is no double maintenance between code and design. When necessary, a document that describes the detailed design of an entire module is created by collecting from the project baseline the skeletons of all the module packages. Each detailed design document contains:

- A decomposition illustration showing packages and interfaces; and

- A skeleton of each package.

Implementation   To implement this strategy for the detailed design phase, the configuration manager must provide:

- A procedure that allows a designer to describe a new package by answering a prescribed set of questions (or filling in a form). The procedure automatically places into the baseline a new package skeleton;

- Procedures that allow designers to read, charge-out, charge-in, and delete packages from the project baseline so that skeletons can be corrected and augmented;

- A procedure that goes through the baseline and collects all the package skeletons for a given module, and collates and formats them into a detailed design document;

- A manual procedure that checks each module decomposition illustration against the design represented by the packages in the baseline; and

■ A procedure (manual or automatic) that compares each interface that a module provides against the matching package skeleton and resolves any inconsistencies.

THE CODING PHASE

The detailed design for a module is finished when its packages are described in complete precision. At this point the project has a baseline containing a skeleton for each package in the module. It is now time to write code.

Goals As in the detailed design phase, an important goal is to minimize divergence between the code and the detailed design for the duration of the project. Another important goal is to structure the code to simplify debugging. This is accomplished by maximizing compile-time checking of conformance to interfaces.

Strategy The first revisions of the source code for each package contain the skeleton that is prepared during detailed design. Now that it is time to code the package, the programmer has available the skeleton, which is a complete outline of the package. He or she writes the code for the package by charging-out the existing source code (the skeleton) and filling in the algorithms of the subroutines. The programmer need not manually copy any design information from any design document.

The strategically placed comments within the skeleton act as reminders to programmers of the expected purpose, side effects, assumptions, error detection, and so on, of the code. The design is in the package, so they can refer to it while they code. The proximity of the comments encourages the programmers to keep them up to date by correcting commentary errors as they find them.

When a package enters the coding phase, a procedure places into the baseline a *specification* file for the package. The specification file is the configuration manager's mechanism for obtaining compile-time checking of conformance to interfaces. Each package specification file contains the definition of the interface provided by the package and is included by other packages that make use of the interface provided.

When using the language C, the specification file contains external declarations of the data and functions that the package provides. The specification file (in C, called a *header*

```
/ *******************************************************
                Specification for PACKAGE buildstack

                      in module rgcontrol


REVISION HISTORY:
    7/15/85     Specification automatically generated from
                package


PURPOSE:
    This package contains routines that control the master
stack. Routines are provided to initialize, push, pop, and
interrogate statistics concerning the stack.*/

/*
SUBROUTINES: */

    /* Function initstack */
    /* Usage: Global subroutine */
    /* Purpose: This subroutine clears the stack */
    /* Side effects: All descriptors on stack are cleanly
       terminated and relevant control blocks deallocated */
    /* Assumptions: Stack contains only valid, active
       descriptors*/
    /* Abnormal exits: to System Diagnosis if stack contains
       invalid entries */
    /* Errors diagnosed: Code 1 if stack has less than zero
       entries */
    /* Definition: */

extern int initstack ()       /* returns error code value*/


            .  .  .
```

Figure 9.5

file) is referenced using *#include* in each package that makes
use of the interface so that the C compiler can make sure
that every variable and function is used in a manner consistent with its type.†

The specification file for the package *buildstack* is shown
in Fig. 9.5. Note that the specification contains only interface, not implementation; in this example, the stack data
structure is not part of the interface.

---

†In the language C, the compiler does not check types of parameters used
in cross-package function calls. This is a handicap the configuration manager has not overcome in this sample project.

Implementation To implement this strategy for the beginning of coding, the configuration manager must provide a procedure that produces a specification for each package and places it into the project baseline.

THE TEST PHASE

After a package is coded, it must be tested. Although coding takes very little time and accounts for a small percentage of the work of the project, testing is time consuming, and a poor testing environment can produce big schedule slips. The measure of the configuration manager's success is how quickly the testing phases progress.

Goals The goals during the testing phases are:

- To continue to minimize divergence between the code and the detailed design;
- To allow programmers to find and fix bugs as quickly as possible by providing a maximum of independence and stability; and
- To build a project baseline containing accurate and internally consistent code, in preparation for eventual delivery.

Strategy Each package is represented in the project baseline by the following three files, which are illustrated in Fig. 9.6.

- The source code;
- The specification; and
- The object code.

The source code and the specification are each revision sets represented by the original and a series of deltas. The object code is present in only one revision, corresponding to the most recent revision of the source code.

The first revisions of the source code and of the specification are created by automatic procedures during the detailed design and coding phases. Later revisions of the source code are created by programmers using charge-out and charge-in. The specification is protected against programmer modification and is charged-out and charged-in only by

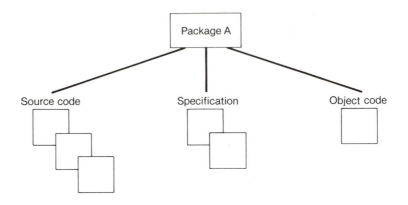

Figure 9.6

the configuration manager. The object code is automatically created by configuration management tools, so it is not charged-in by the programmers.

When programmers want to change source code in one or more packages, they charge them out, and copies are placed into their private workspace for editing. They may edit the copies and are expected to test changes thoroughly before performing a charge-in.

To provide themselves with a completely stable test environment, programmers copy in all specifications that their packages reference and object code for all modules with which they are linked. They then compile and link wholly within their workspace as many times as necessary and are guaranteed stability even if specifications or source code in the baseline are revised.

After they believe their edits are correct, they will want to test against the current baseline (rather than the copies in their own workspace) before charging-in their revised package. To do this, they compile their packages, referencing the most recent specifications present in the baseline, then link with the baseline object code for the other packages. They may now execute tests, confident that they are testing against the most recent project software, then charge-in their packages.

It is possible that while coding or debugging, programmers will detect errors that require corrections to the design. They might, for example, note that a comment fails to list all errors detected or insufficiently describes the purpose of a parameter. If the changes don't affect the package specification, programmers are expected to make corrections to the comments as they code. In this manner, the configuration manager encourages the programmer to keep the design up-to-date by allowing them to change the design at the same time they change the code.

Other design changes are not so easy to correct. While coding or debugging a package, programmers might decide that changes to the package specifications are necessary. Programmers are not permitted to change the specification directly or change the package source code in a way that contradicts its established specification. To change the specification, programmers use a manual procedure described later in this section.

The procedure for charging-in source code for one or more packages works like this:

1. For each package, the new source code is compared to its specification to make sure that programmers haven't changed anything that would put the source code in conflict with the specification. If there is a conflict, all the source code is rejected, and programmers repair the source code so that it no longer conflicts or resort to a manual procedure to change the specification.

2. The new source code is compiled using the most recent revisions of any *included* specifications, and all the new source code is rejected if any compilation fails.

3. The resultant object code is linked with the other object code present in the baseline.

4. A few tests are submitted against the resultant executable load image, and the test results are automatically examined. If any of the tests fails, all the new package source code is rejected.

5. The programmer provides a change-log entry for each new source code, describing the changes he or she made.

6. A new revision for each package source code is created and saved in the baseline with each newly compiled object code, along with their corresponding derivation histories.

The small amount of regression testing performed by the charge-in procedure is not a substitute for full qualification testing nor for thorough testing by programmers before charge-in. This testing serves to keep the entire project from being roadblocked by an unfortunate "foolish" mistake that prevents the package from fulfilling even its most basic functions.

If it is necessary to change a specification, programmers use a manual procedure that seeks consent from concerned people and results in the configuration manager personally charging-out, editing, and charging-in the revised specification. (Only the configuration manager may charge-in a specification.)

A modification to a specification might require changes to the source code of packages that reference the specification. (A new parameter added to a subroutine definition, for example, requires a new argument in every call.) If such changes are necessary, the configuration manager gathers the necessary changes from the responsible programmers so that all may be introduced into the baseline at once. In this way, the configuration manager maintains the internal consistency and correctness of the baseline.

When a specification is changed, object code is potentially incorrect for every package that makes use of (*includes*) the specification. This is possible even for packages whose source code requires no modification (such as when the type of a record field is changed). So when a new revision of a specification is charged-in by the configuration manager, a special charge-in procedure automatically recompiles all affected packages, creating new object code for each. Because of the volume of computer resources required, the configuration manager typically charges-in a heavily used specification only at off-peak hours.

Implementation   To support the programming staff during the test phases, the configuration manager must provide procedures to allow programmers to perform these tasks:

- Charge-out and charge-in source code for packages, as described in the preceding paragraphs;
- Copy, on a read-only basis, specifications and object code into their private workspaces for testing;
- Compile and link packages against specifications and object code present in their workspaces; and
- Compile and link packages against the most recent copies of specifications and object code present in the baseline.

These procedures must also be provided:

- A manual procedure for proposing and seeking approval for changes to package specifications; and
- Procedures, restricted for use only by the configuration manager, for charging-out and charging-in package specifications and their associated changed source code,

making sure that the new source code and the new specification agree, and making sure that all invalid object code in the baseline is replaced by newly compiled object code. (Since the project is using Unix, the *make* tool might be used to implement this procedure.)

QA, DELIVERY, AND MAINTENANCE

As delivery nears, the testing process becomes more formal and the project seeks quality assurance (QA) certification. It is now necessary to identify, track, and fix bugs in an organized manner so management can decide when to deliver to the customer. After the first delivery, bugs will continue to be identified. The customer will expect revised deliveries in which these bugs are fixed and new functions are provided.

Goals　The configuration manager's goals during these phases are:

■　To continue to maintain the accuracy and consistency of the project baseline, including source code, object code, and specifications;

■　To keep track of which bugs have and have not been fixed;

■　To prepare customer deliveries that reflect the best state of the software; and

■　To continue to allow programmers to find and fix bugs and to add new features as quickly as possible with a maximum of independence and stability.

Strategy　The project continues to use the charge-in, charge-out, compiling, linking, and other procedures that are provided for the earlier testing phases. Additional procedures provide bug tracking.

In this phase of the project, programmers no longer make changes to the baseline on their own initiative; they make changes only in response to reported bugs. Bugs are reported to the configuration manager by the testing organization, by the customers, or by the programmers themselves.

For each bug that is reported, the configuration manager prepares a *bug report*, which contains a description of the bug and a list of tests that fail due to the bug. The configuration manager keeps a log of all bug reports, both *open* (when the bug is unfixed) and *closed* (when the bug has been fixed). Figure 9.7 shows a sample bug report form. The bug reports are identified with a serial number assigned by the configuration manager.

To fix bugs, the programmer locates the error and charges-out and edits the source code, using normal testing and baseline management procedures. After making the necessary changes in the workspace, the programmer performs the tests that previously failed, making sure they now pass. He or she then charges-in new revisions of the fixed packages and records in the change logs the number of the bug report that prompted the change.

On the bug report form, the programmer describes the cause of the bug and the packages he or she repaired. The programmer shows which new revisions of source code and specifications were created to remove the bug.

To be sure the bug is fixed, the configuration manager prepares a load image from the most current object code in the baseline and performs the tests that previously failed to make sure that they now pass. Then the bug is officially declared dead and the bug report is closed.

The configuration manager gives the project management a periodic summary of outstanding and fixed bugs,

Figure 9.7

```
                            BUG REPORT

NUMBER: _____ Priority ___ Date discovered _____
Bug ___; Requirements change ___; Performance improvement ___;
Description: _____
_____
Possible reasons: _____
_____
Tests that demonstrate the bug:
            _____        _____
            _____        _____
            _____        _____
Fixed by: _____ Date fixed _____
Actual cause of bug: _____
_____
Packages repaired:
      Source code:      _____ New revision #: _____
      Source code:      _____ New revision #: _____
      Source code:      _____ New revision #: _____
      Specification: _____ New revision #: _____
      Specification: _____ New revision #: _____
Tests passed against baseline date _____ by _____
```

perhaps categorizing the bugs by priority or by the nature of functionality they impact. The summary allows management to decide when the software is or will be ready for delivery, and where resources should be concentrated to fix the most important bugs.

When it comes time to deliver the software, the configuration manager prepares a load image using the most recent object code in the baseline. The load image is thoroughly tested by QA, and, if it passes, is delivered to customers. The configuration manager carefully prepares a special derivation history, called a *version description document,* for the load image. The version description document shows:

■ The revision numbers of all package source codes and specifications that are represented in the configuration. This information, together with the lists of tools and parameters used to compile and link, allows the load image to be reproduced if necessary;

■ The list of all bug reports still outstanding (unfixed) in the load image; and

■ A comprehensive list of differences between this customer delivery and the last one, including bugs that have been fixed and features that have been added.

During the maintenance of the software, customers will expect, in addition to bug fixes, new or different functions to be added. If the changes necessary for new functions are localized and quick to implement, they can be tracked and implemented using the bug-tracking mechanism. A report can be initiated showing the desired change, and a programmer can be assigned to make the correction for inclusion in the next delivery.

Many times, however, new functions affect a large number of packages and take a long time to build. In that case, it is inappropriate to use ordinary charge-out and charge-in protocols because a large number of packages would be charged-out and locked against access by other programmers for a long time. Rather than force other progress to grind to a halt while the new feature is implemented, the configuration manager provides procedures that allow for *parallel* development efforts.

To allow for parallel development, the configuration manager allows the team working on new features to create variations of packages they plan to modify. Since a special variation is available for new-feature development, the package need not be locked against concurrent access by the rest of the programming team.

The representation of a typical package in the baseline might now look like Fig. 9.8.

The single sequence of revisions for the package is forked into two variations, one for each of the parallel developments. The team working on the new functionality (development path 2) has one revision series, whereas the rest of the team (development path 1) has its own parallel series.

The package illustrated has dual variations for the source code and specification. Other packages may have only the source code varied, but not the specification, or might have nothing varied at all (implying that the package is identical in both development groups). If a particular package is not affected by the new functionality, there is no parallel revision series, and any changes made to the package are automatically available to both paths with no need for double maintenance.

Though the source code and specification need not be varied, there will be two variations of the object code for every package. Even if the source code and specification for a package are identical for the two development paths, it is possible that the package *includes* a specification that is varied, in which case object code for the two paths can differ.

In Fig. 9.9, the source code for package B *includes* specifications for A and C. The source code for package B has not been varied, because it is the same for both development paths. The object code for B, however, is present in two

Figure 9.8

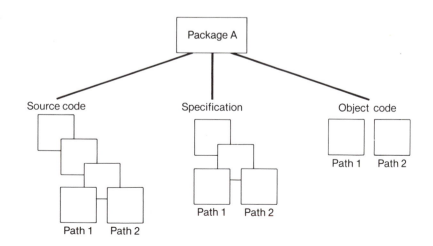

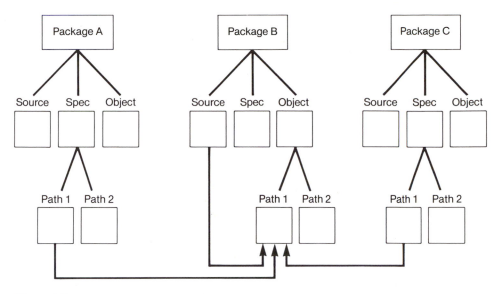

Figure 9.9

variations. The path 1 object code is prepared by compiling the package using the path 1 variations of A's and C's specifications, whereas the path 2 object code is compiled using the path 2 variations of the specifications.

To support the variations of source code, specifications, and object code, the configuration manager provides different sets of baseline management procedures, one for each of the development paths. For example, the path 2 team will have a special procedure to vary source code or specification when they decide it is necessary to change it. Their charge-out procedure will forbid them to charge-out a package until they have varied it.

The source code charge-in procedure for path 2 does the following:

1. Compares the new source code against the path 2 variation of the package specification to make sure specification and source code do not conflict;

2. Compiles the new source code using the most recent revisions of the path 2 specifications;

3. Links the resultant object code with other path 2 object code;

4. Performs special tests for path 2 against the resultant executable load image (special path 2 tests are necessary because path 2 has different functionality than path 1);

5. Accepts from the programmer a change-log entry for the new source code; and

6. Saves in the baseline a new revision for the path 2 variation of the source code and the newly compiled path 2 object code.

When members of path 2 charge-out a package, they receive the most recent revision of the path's variation. When they compile, the compiler *includes* the path 2 variation of each specification they reference. When they link, the linker uses only the path 2 object codes for all the packages. The two development paths can now operate in a nearly complete isolation, with neither path's progress inhibited by activities of the other development team.

Eventually, the development of the new functionality will be complete. The teams are now ready to merge their development paths in preparation for a new delivery that includes both the new functionality (developed in path 2) and the bug fixes and enhancements (developed in path 1). The process of merging development paths is semiautomatic, but still time-consuming. It takes advantage of the baseline deltas that are used to represent the differences between revisions.

For each package whose source code has been varied, a programmer is assigned to merge the development paths. The programmer starts with the most recent revision of one of the development paths (for example, the most recent revision of path 1) and applies all the deltas that have been applied along path 2 to introduce the path 2 changes into the path 1 software.

In the example in Fig. 9.10, there are two deltas to be applied. The programmer charges-out path 1 rev 5, then applies the delta that transformed rev 2 into path 2 rev 3, then applies the delta that transformed path 2 rev 3 into path 2 rev 4. The finished product, called rev 6, is a package that merges the changes from the two paths.

The application of the deltas is automatic, but it is manually supervised because of the likelihood that some changes that are appropriate along one development path are inappropriate along the other. The programmer inspects each line that is changed to make sure the change is correct, then thoroughly tests the merged package to check the work.

When all packages have been merged, the parallel development is over.

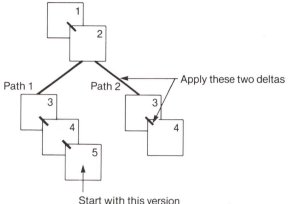

Figure 9.10

Start with this version

Implementation   To support the programming staff during QA, Delivery, and Maintenance, the configuration manager provides the following:

- A procedure for creating a new bug report, including entering the bug in the configuration manager's log for tracking and status reporting;

- A procedure for closing a bug report, including appropriate testing of the fix;

- Periodic reports on the status and number of bugs, categorized in the manner specified by management;

- A version description document for each software delivery;

- Capabilities in the baseline to support dual object code for each package, in support of parallel development paths;

- A procedure to vary a package source code, specification, or description, in support of parallel development paths;

- Improved procedures for charge-out, charge-in, compiling, linking, and copying, to support parallel development paths; and

- Semiautomatic procedures for merging parallel development paths, including automatic application of deltas from one path to a revision on the other path.

Recommended Reading

General

Two books are essential reading for the student of communication and coordination in a software development team. Both are acknowledged classics:

Brooks, F. P., Jr. *The Mythical Man-Month*. Reading, Mass.: Addison-Wesley, 1975.

The principle of mythical man-months is so widely quoted as part of the folklore that many people don't know where the idea came from. (The classic quote is "Adding manpower to a late software project makes it later.") This book is an original, well-written, and insightful presentation of the problem of communication among members of a programming team and the dangers of a large staff.

Weinberg, G. M. *The Psychology of Computer Programming*. New York: Van Nostrand Reinhold, 1971.

Configuration management is not only a technical problem but also a social and psychological one. The issues of how programmers think together, work together, and make progress together are explored in this landmark book. See if you can find the renegades in Weinberg's vingnettes.

Interfaces

Parnas' principles of information hiding were originally discussed in a university technical report that might be hard to obtain. Later descriptions have appeared in more widely circulated periodicals.

Parnas, D. L. "Information distribution aspects of design methodology." Technical Report, Dept. of Computer Science, Carnegie-Mellon University, Feb. 1971. Also published in the *Proceedings of IFIP Congress, 1971, Ljubljana, Yugloslavia.*

———. "On the Criteria to be Used in Decomposing Systems into Modules." *Communications of the ACM.* Vol. 15, No. 12 (Dec. 1972).

The presentation of interface diagrams and hierarchical decomposition in Chapter 4 is loosely adapted from other more formally defined design methodologies such as Structured Analysis and Design Tool (SADT), discussed by Ross and Brackett, and Module Interconnection Language (MIL), discussed by DeRemer and Kron.

Ross, D. T., and Brackett, J. W. "An Approach to Structured Analysis." *Computer Decisions* Vol. 8, No. 9 (1976).

DeRemer, F., and Kron, H. H. "Programming-in-the-Large Versus Programming-in-the-Small." *IEEE Transactions on Software Engineering* Vol. SE-2, No. 2 (June 1976).

Tools

The Unix configuration management tools (discussed in Chapter 7) are described in documentation provided with the software and also in the following publications:

Feldman, S. I., "Make—A program for Maintaining Computer Programs." *Software—Practice and Experience* Vol. 9, No. 4 (April 1979).

Rochkind, M. J. "The Source Code Control System." *IEEE Transactions on Software Engineering* Vol. SE-1, No. 4 (Dec. 1975).

Tichy, W. F. "Design, Implementation, and Evaluation of a Revision Control System." *Proceedings of the 6th International Conference on Software Engineering* (Sept. 1982).

The Ada Language System capabilities for configuration management (discussed in Chapter 8) are presented in:

Thall, R. "Large Scale Software Development with the Ada Language System." *Proceedings of the Eleventh Annual Computer Science Conference*, Association for Computing Machinery (Feb. 1983).

SofTech, Inc. *Ada Language System Textbook*, Document 1102–9.2. Waltham, Mass.: SofTech, Inc., Dec. 1984.

For descriptions of other production systems that support serious configuration management software, see Leblang and Chase, who describe the Domain Software Engineering Environment (DSEE) available on Apollo workstations. A product brief is also available from the manufacturer, Apollo Computers, Chelmsford, Mass. Also see The Digital Equipment Corporation Manual that describes VAX CMS/MMS.

Leblang, D. B., and R. P. Chase Jr. "Computer-Aided Software Engineering in a Distributed Workstation Environment." *ACM SIGPLAN/SIGSOFT Symposium on Practical Software Development Environments* (April 1984).

Digital Equipment Corp., *CMS/MMS: Code/Module Management System Manual*, Maynard, Mass. (1982).

Index